I0474379

Real World

Colouring Book

For Advanced Users & Adults

50 Images

Created From Real Life Photos For You To Colour As You Please.

ISBN 978-0-359-86521-5
90000
9 780359 865215

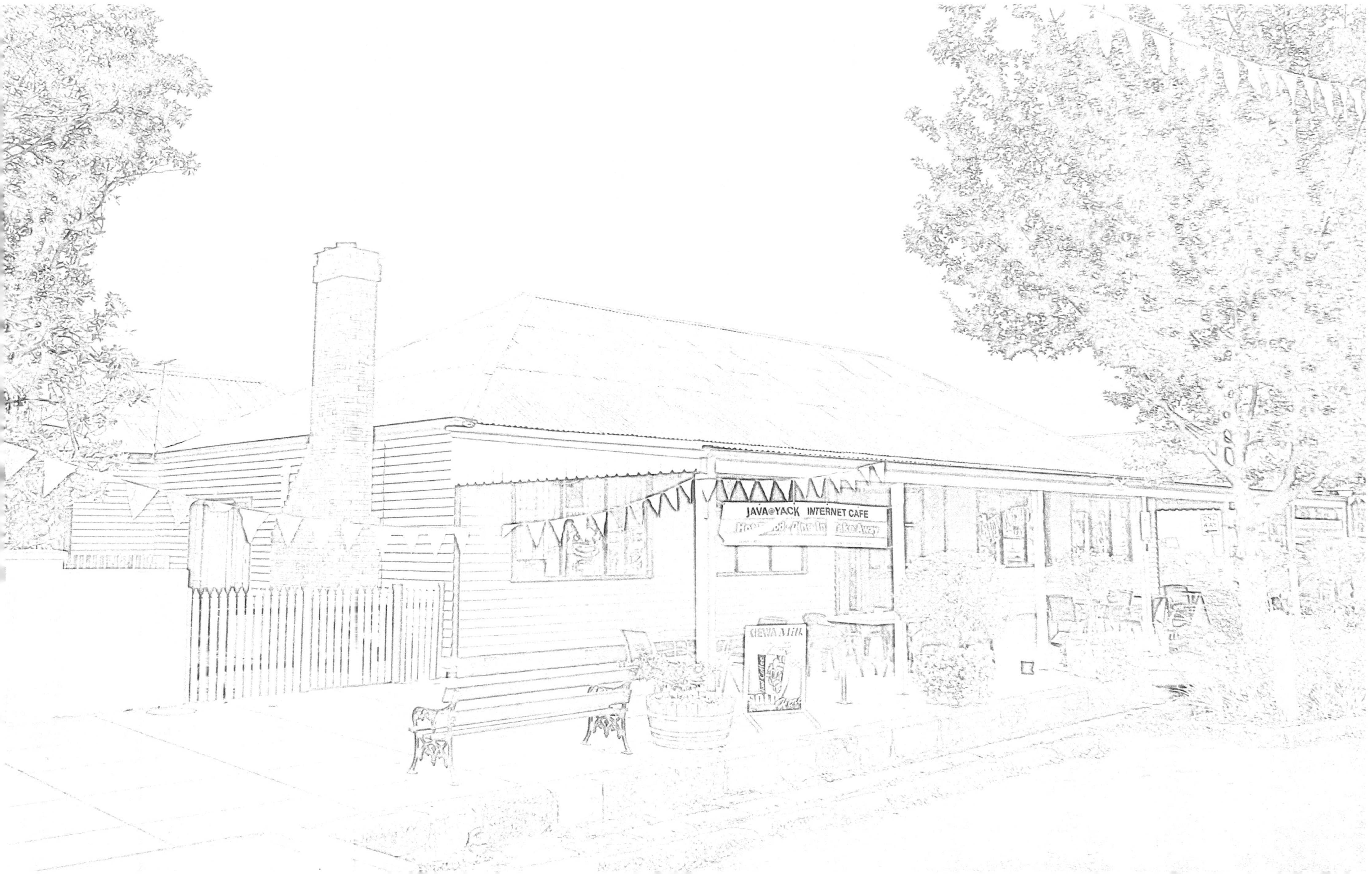
JAVA@YACK INTERNET CAFE
KIEWA Milk

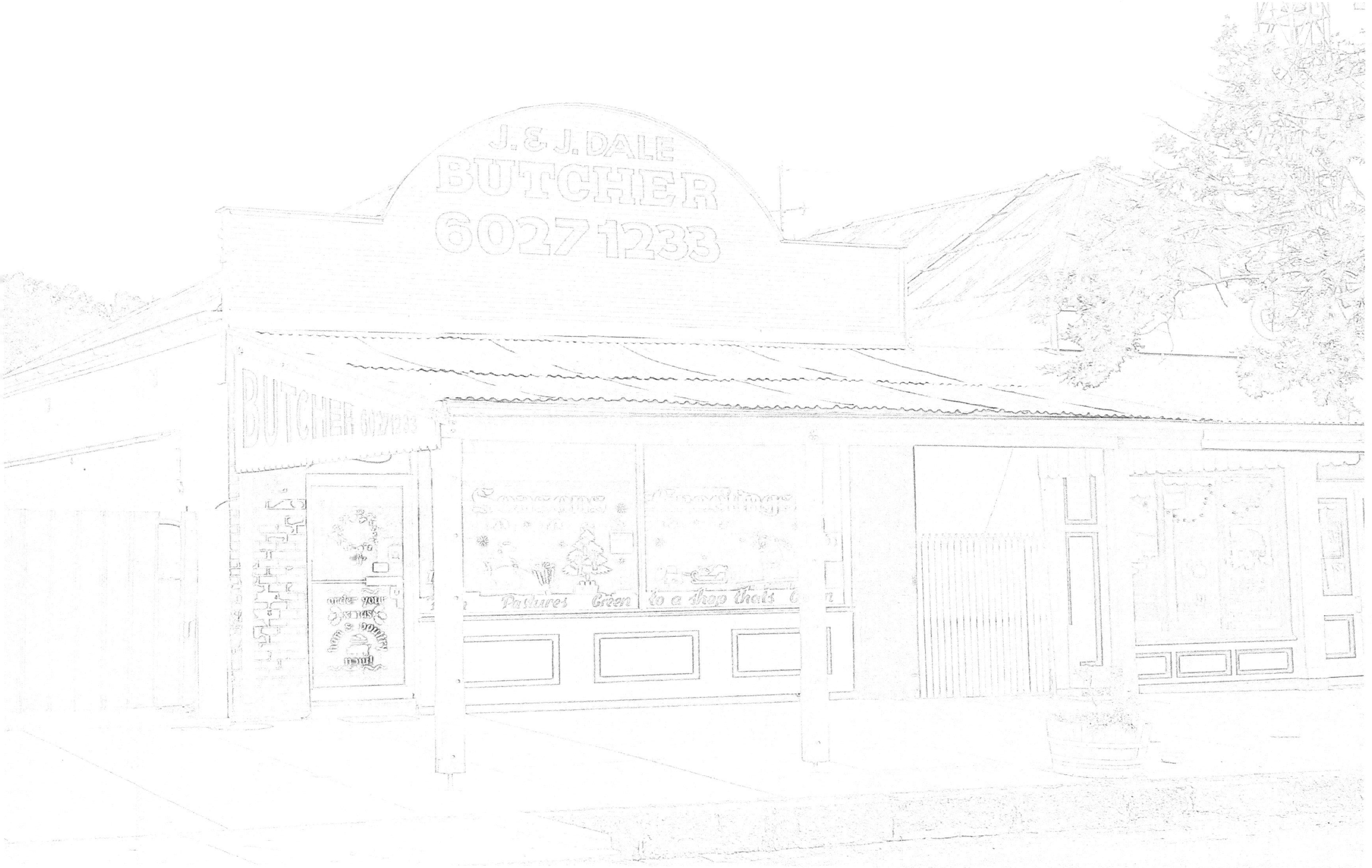
J. & J. DALE
BUTCHER
6027 1233
BUTCHER 6027 1233
Pastures Green
to a shop thats
order your
x mas
ham & poultry
now!

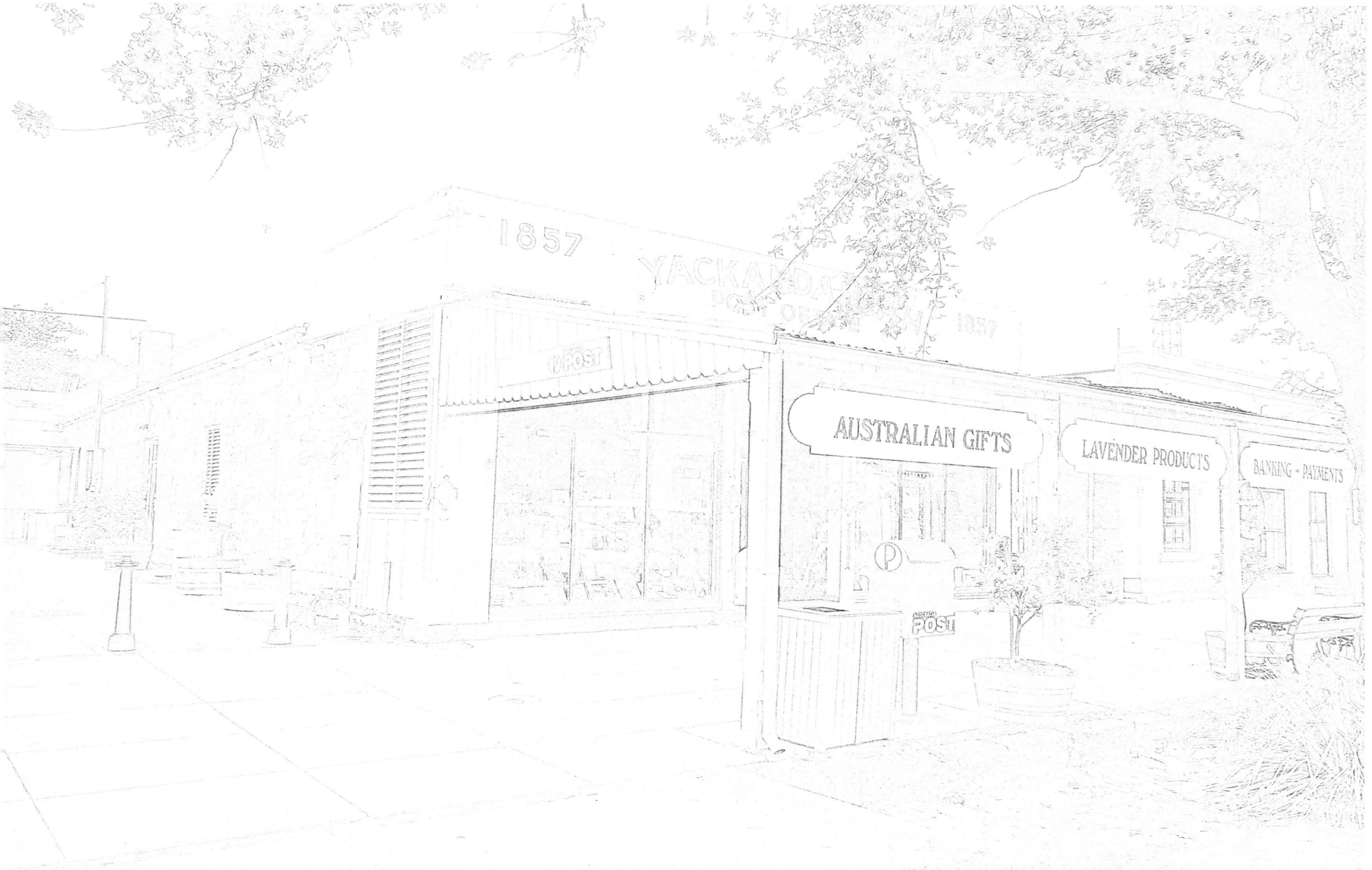

1857
POST
1857
AUSTRALIAN GIFTS
LAVENDER PRODUCTS
BANKING - PAYMENTS
POST

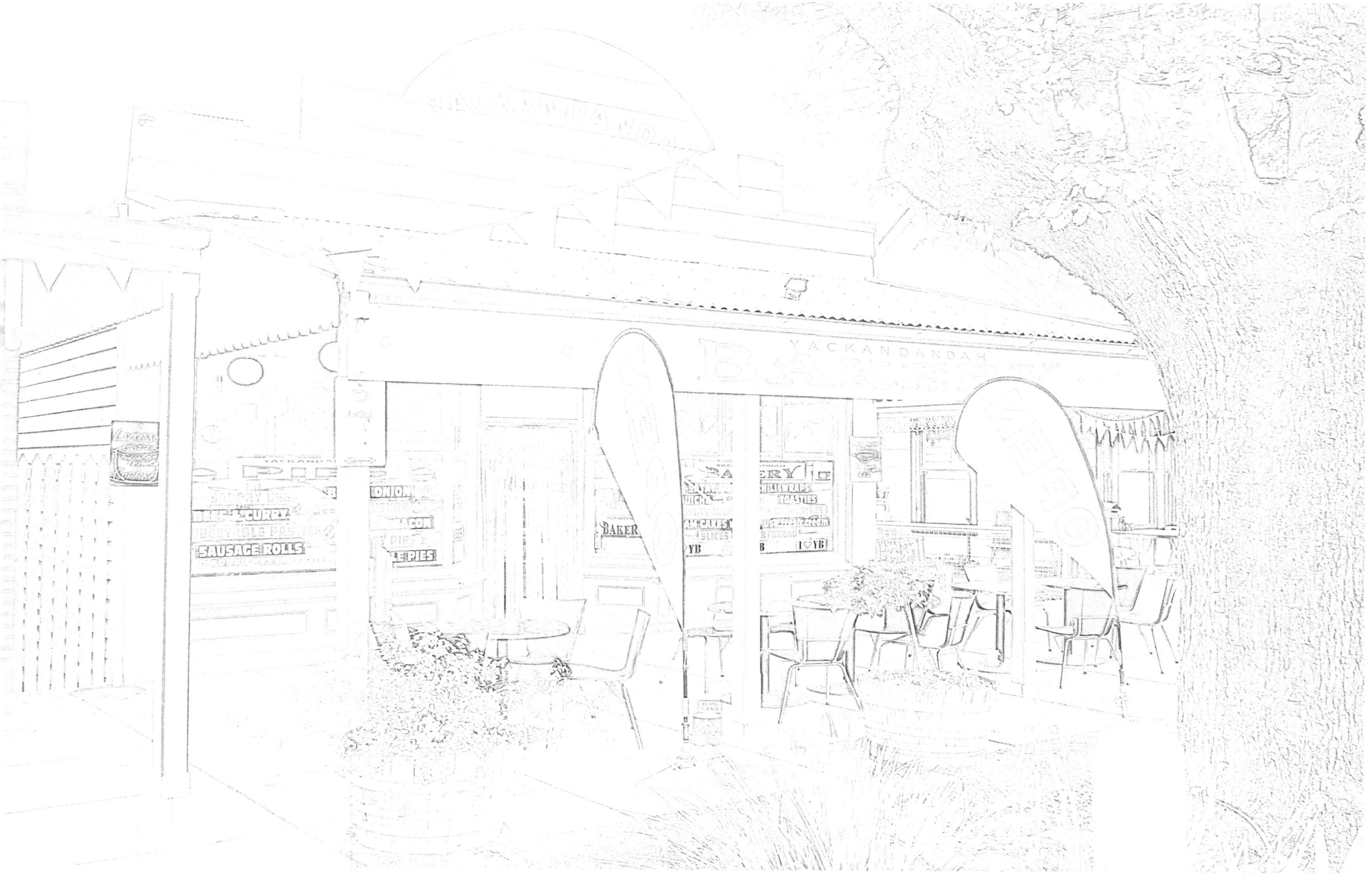
YACKANDANDAH
ONION
SAUSAGE ROLLS
I ♥ YB

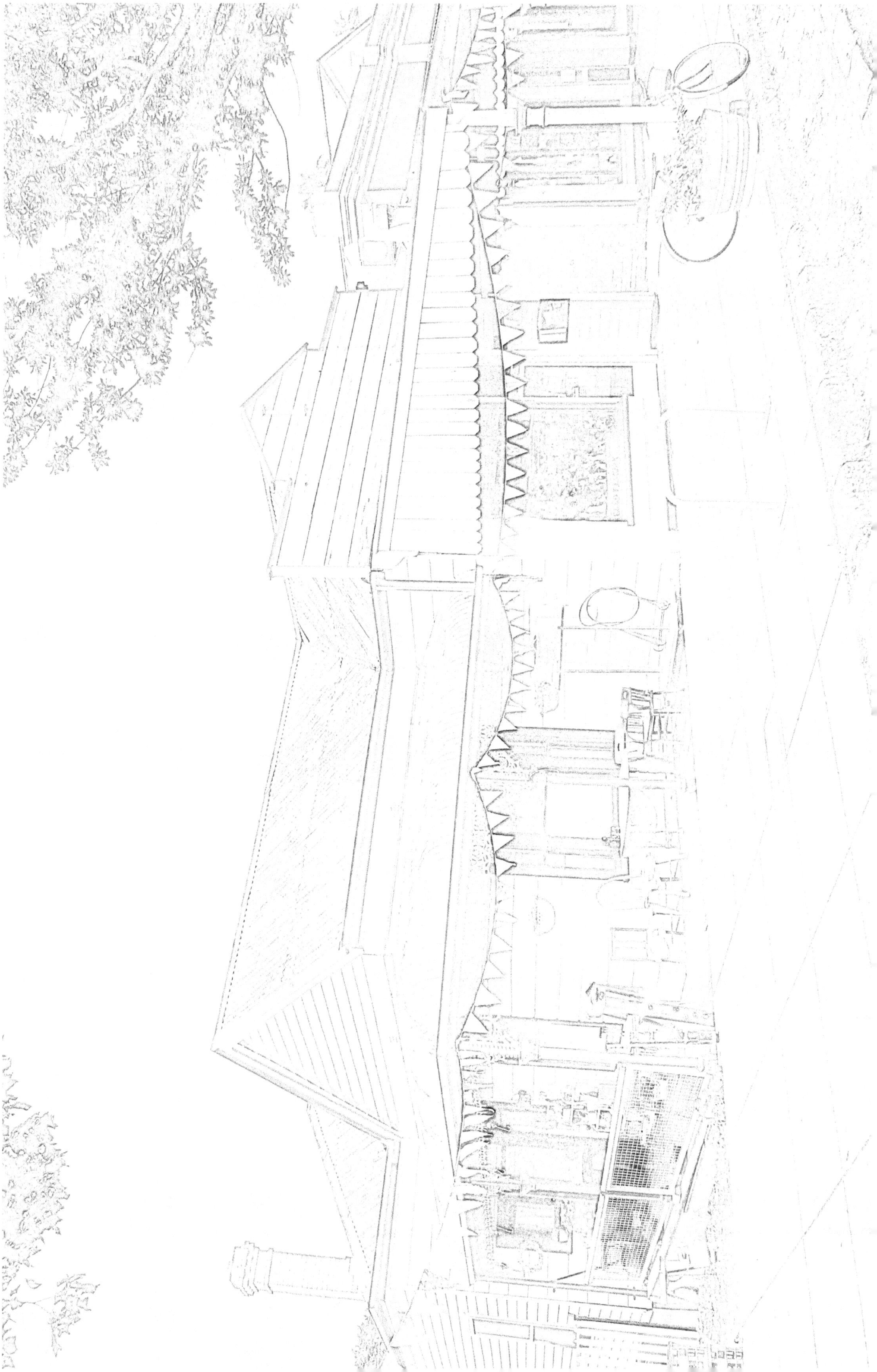

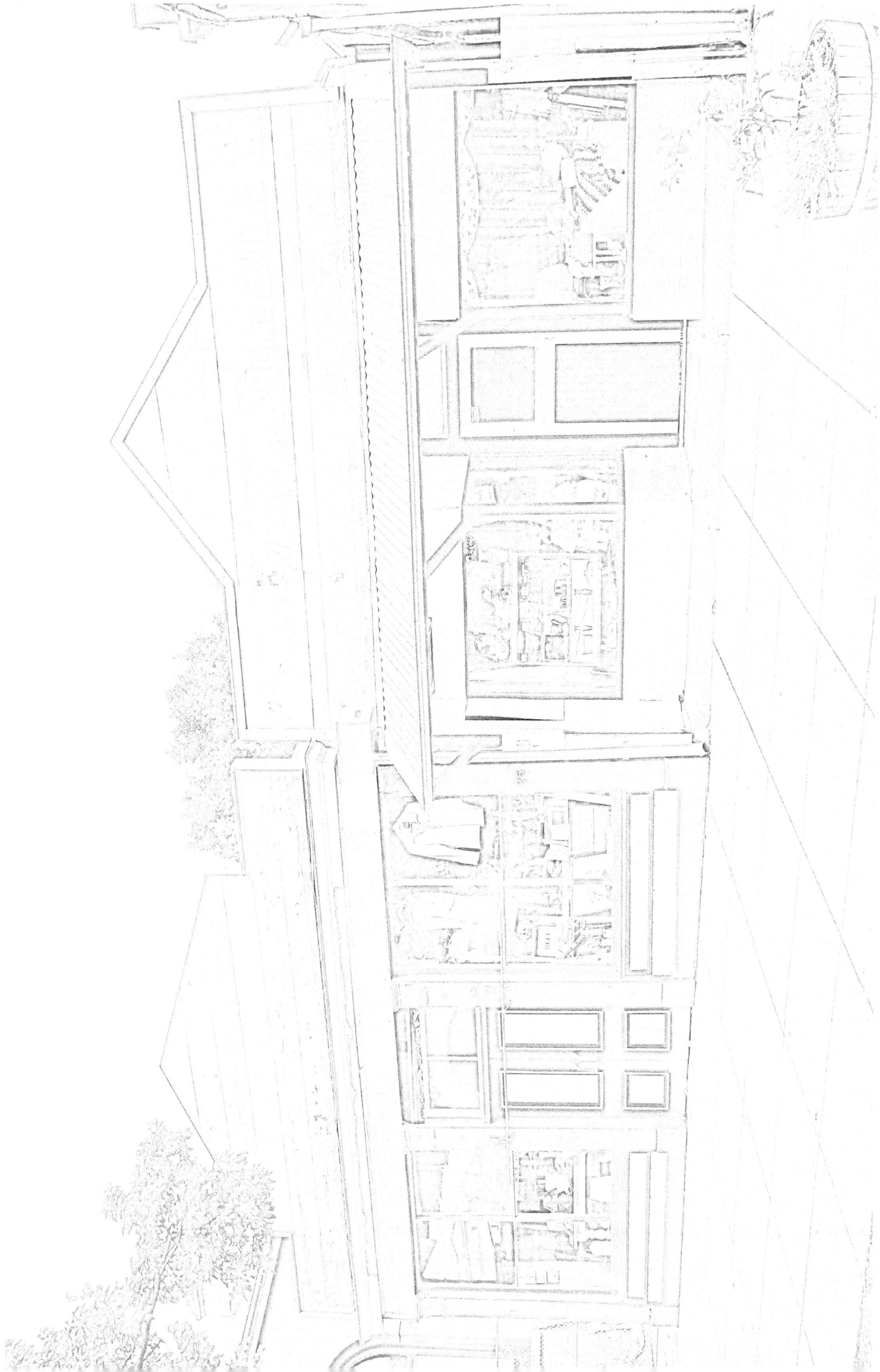

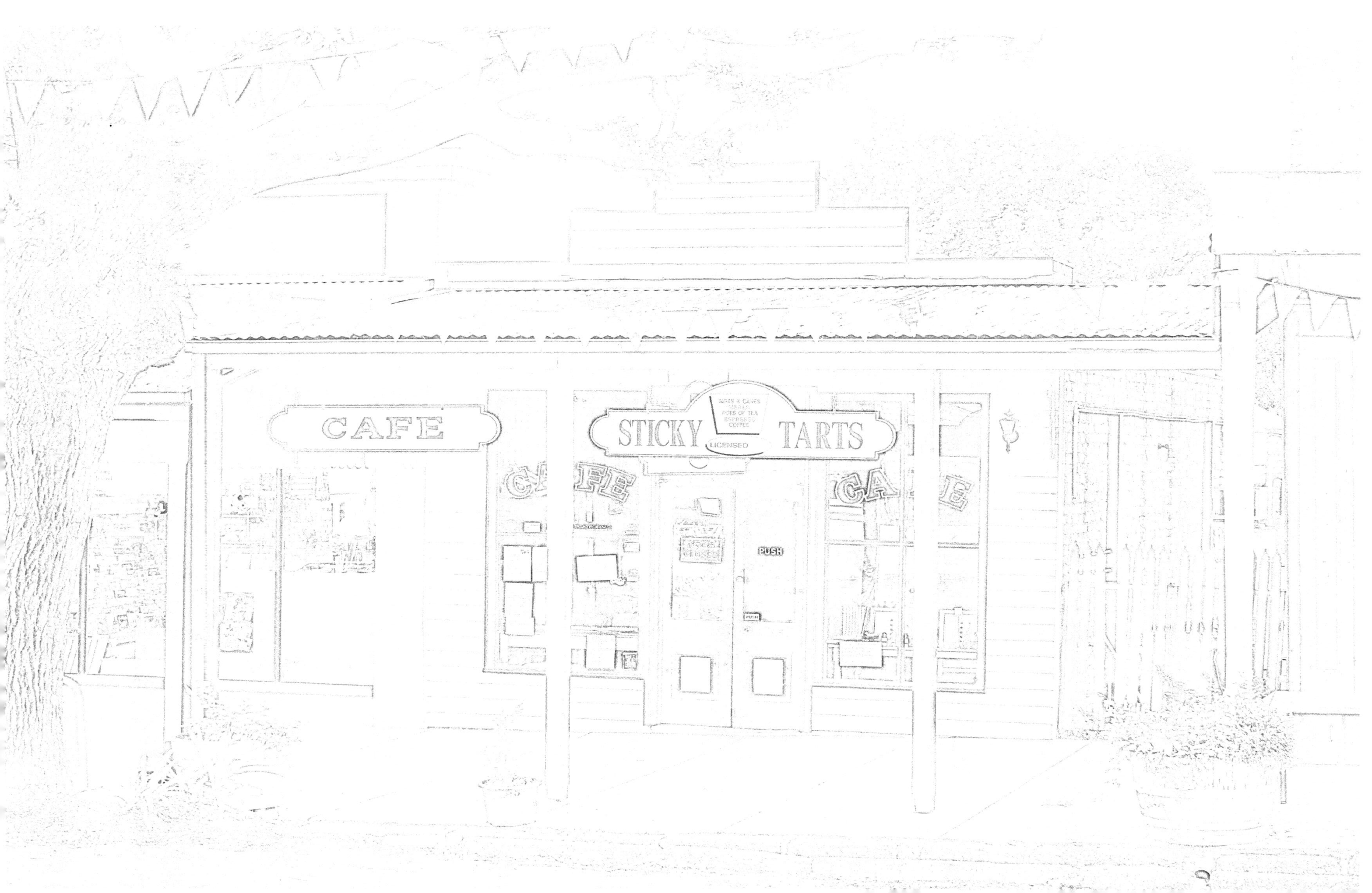
CAFE
STICKY TARTS
LICENSED
TARTS & CAKES
POTS OF TEA
ESPRESSO COFFEE
CAFE
CAFE
PUSH

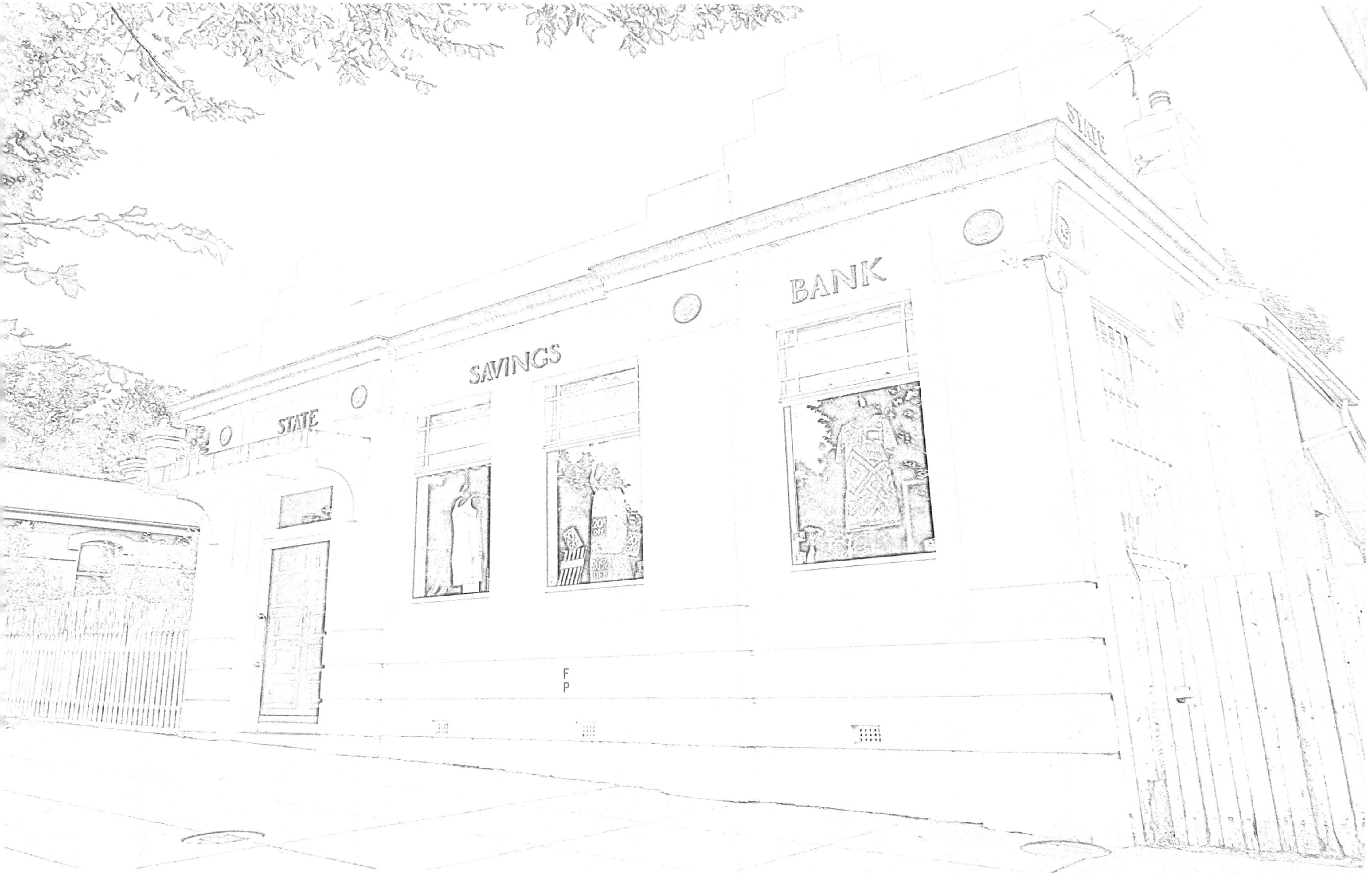
STATE SAVINGS BANK
STATE
F
P

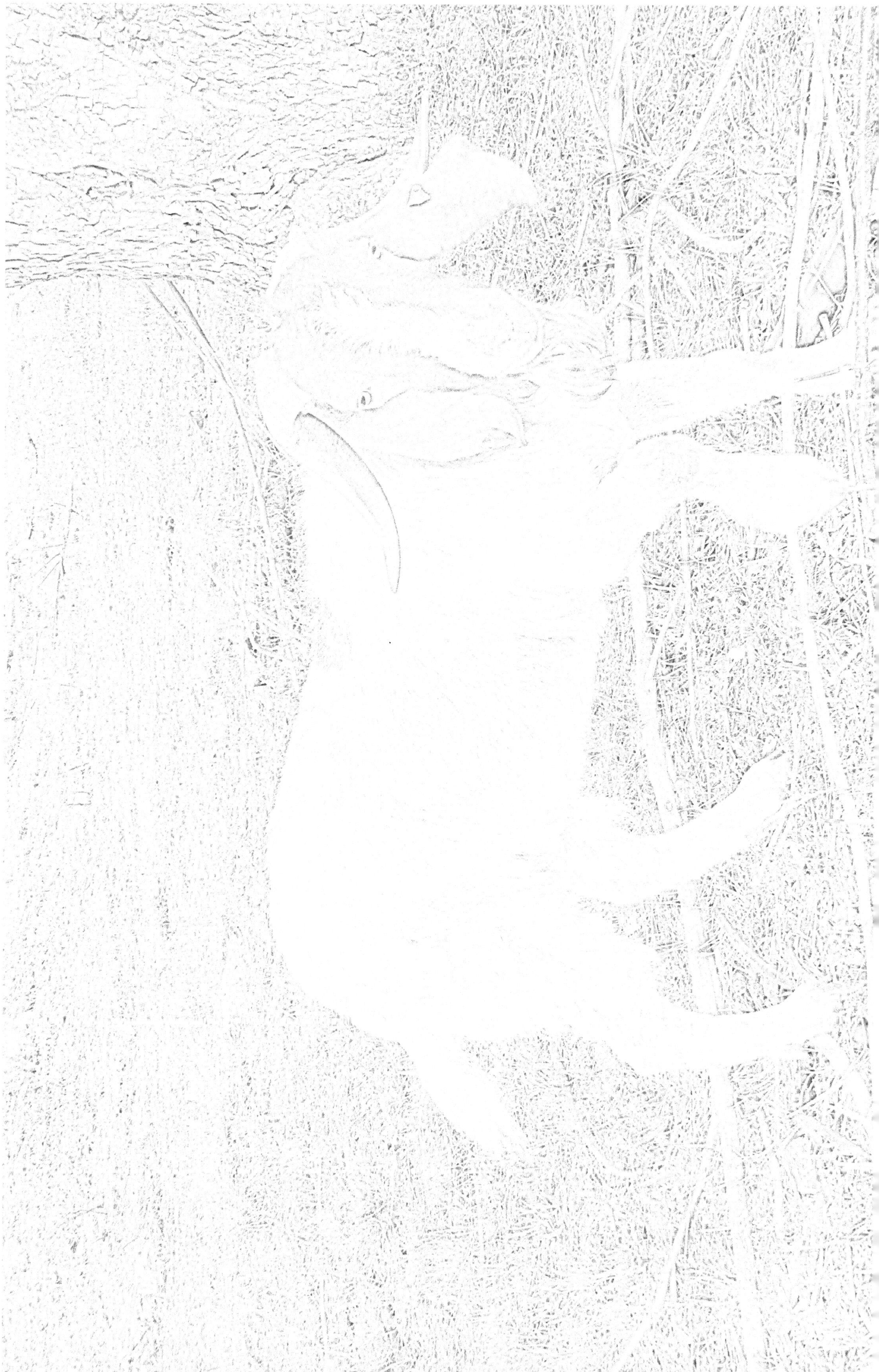

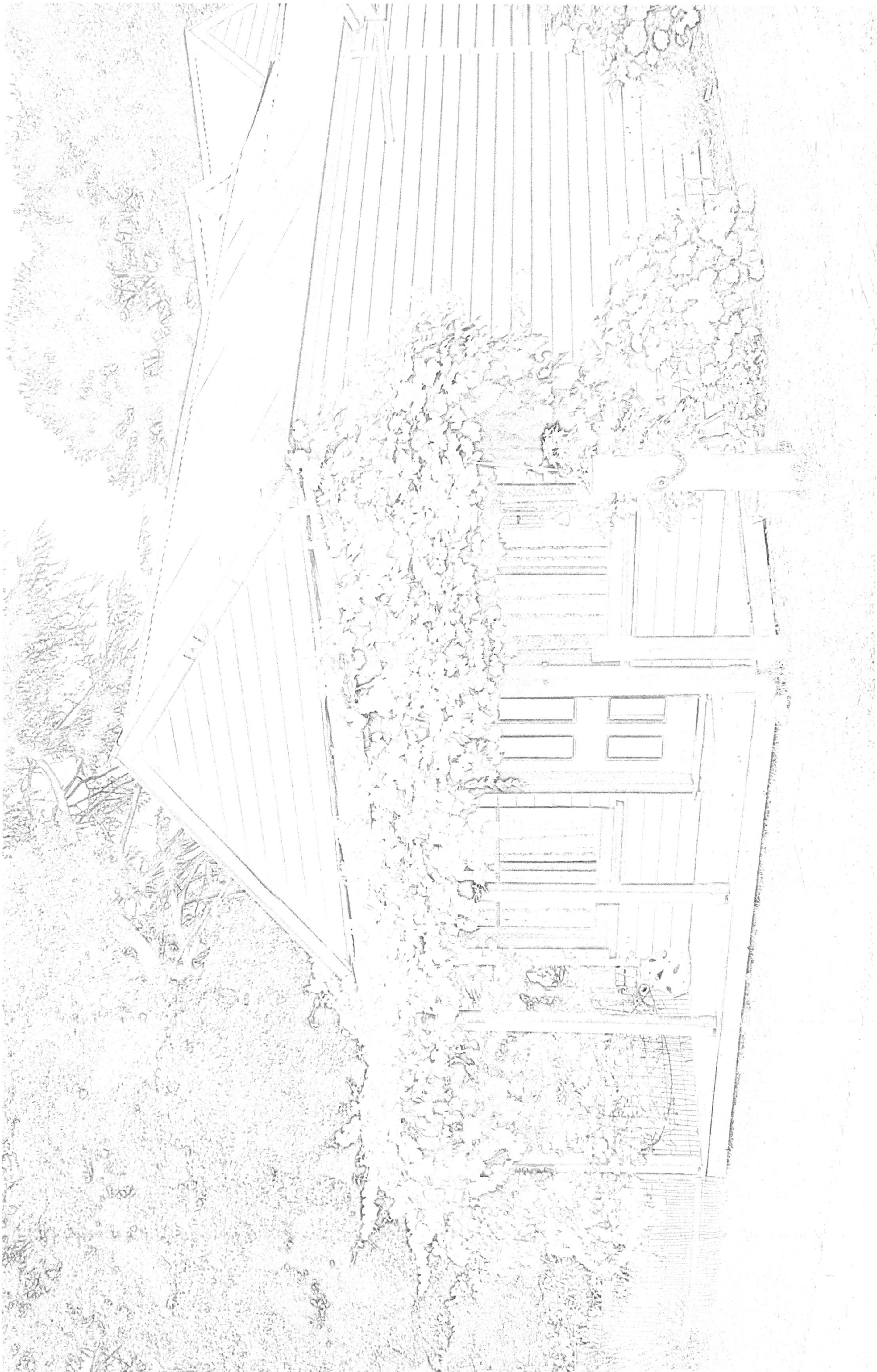

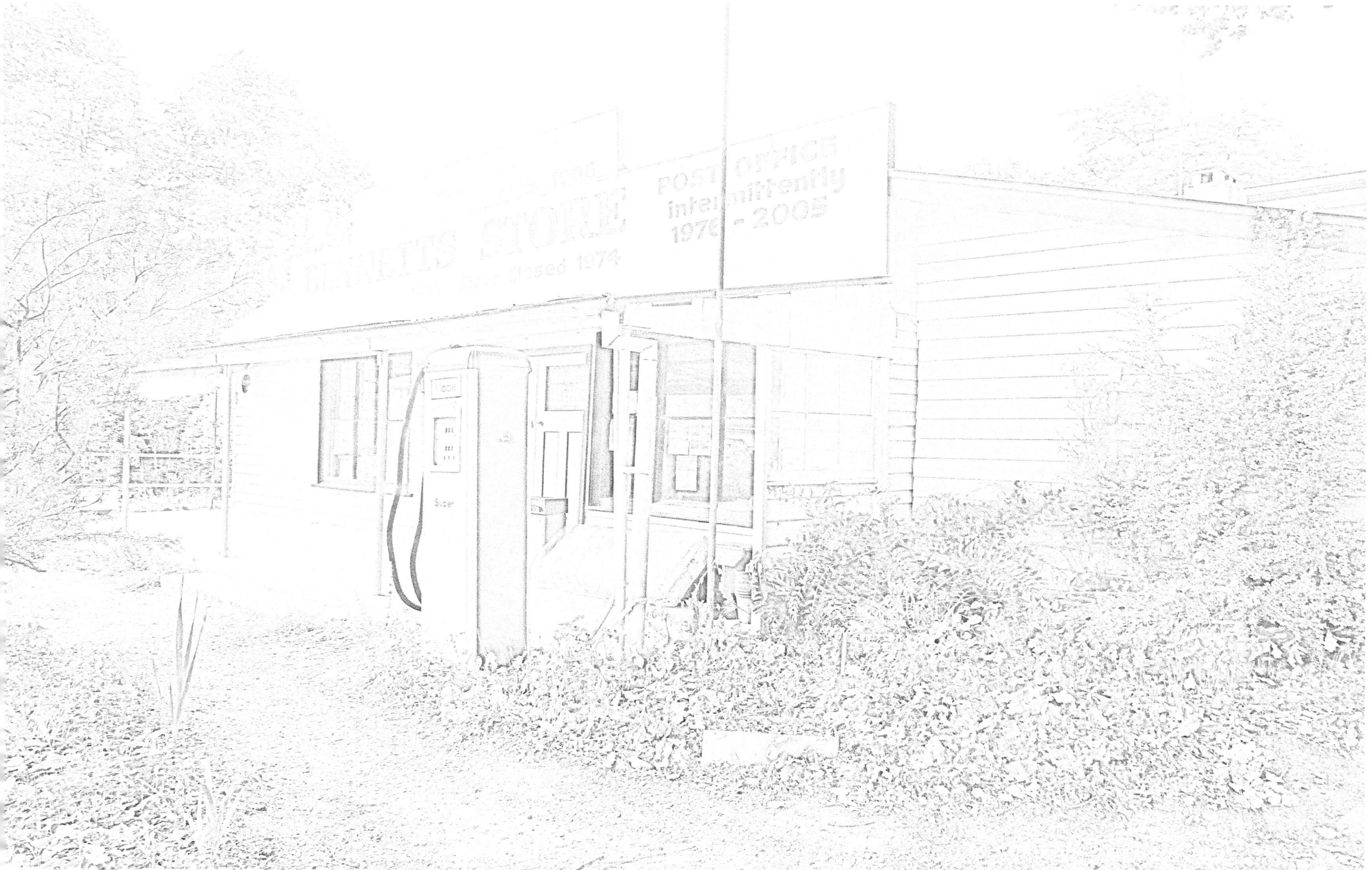
BENNETTS STORE
Closed 1974
POST OFFICE
intermittently
1976 - 2005
Super

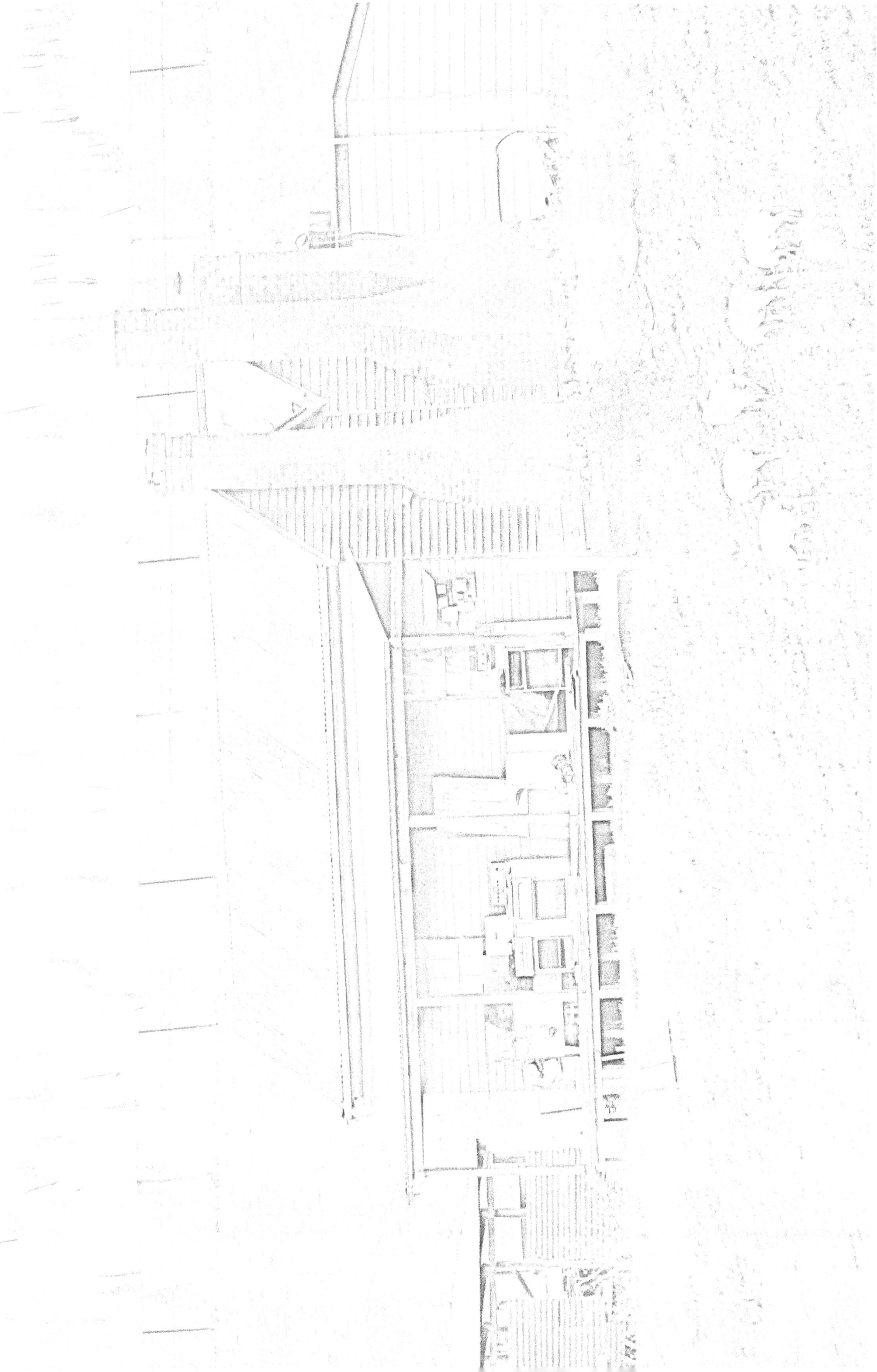

1891
South Gippsland
Creamery
and
Butter Factory
Company L^{td}

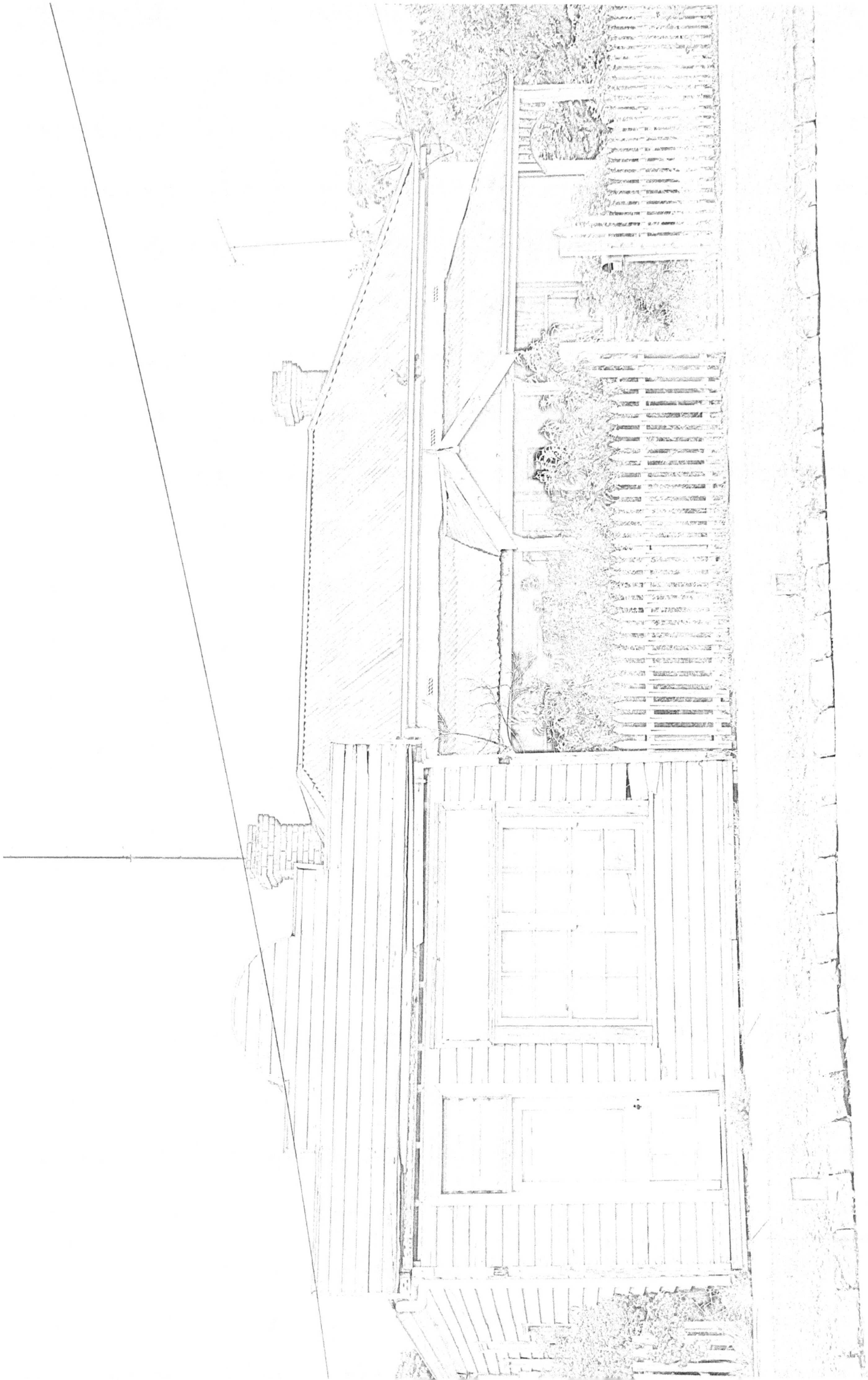

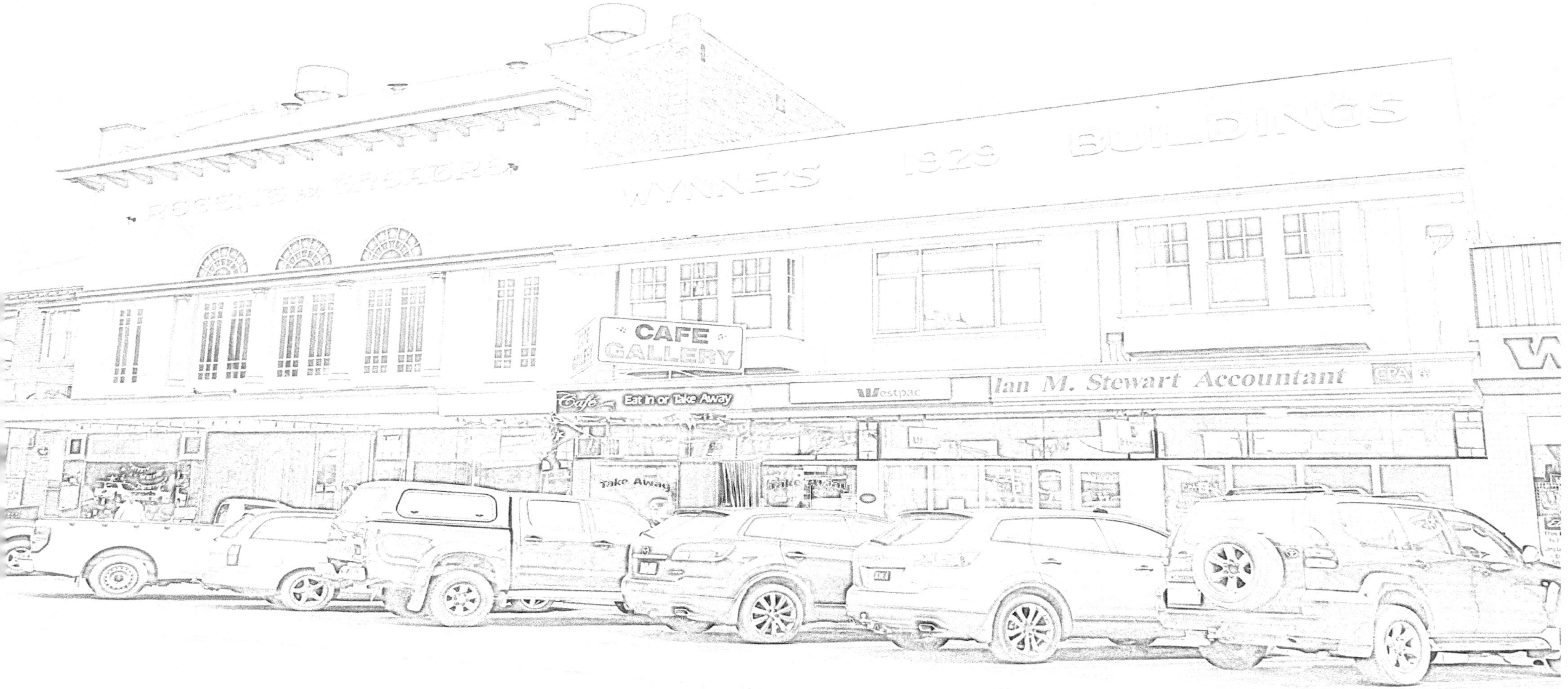
WYNNE'S 1929 BUILDINGS
CAFE GALLERY
Café Eat In or Take Away
Westpac
Ian M. Stewart Accountant
CPA
Take Away

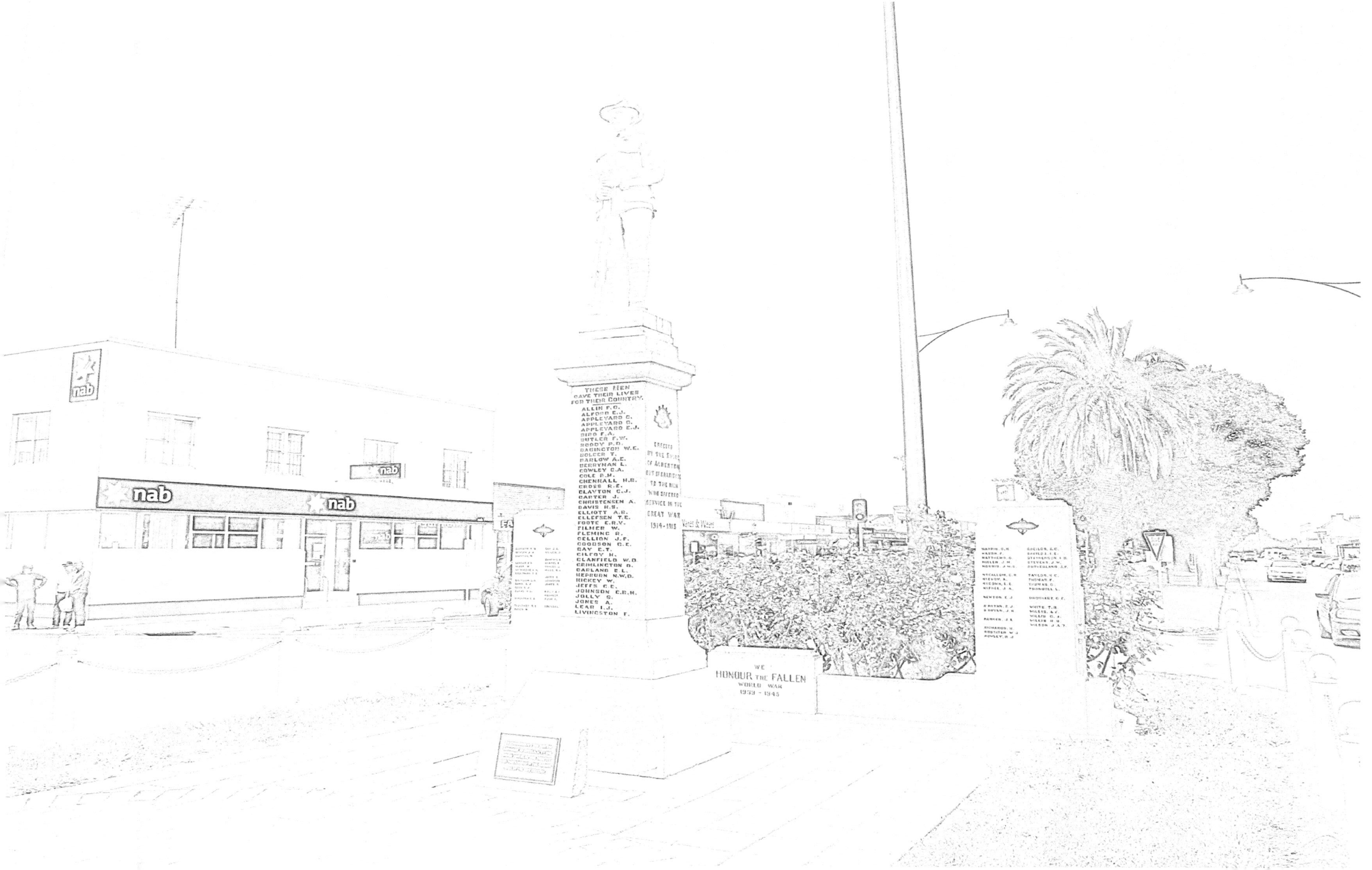
nab
nab
nab
nab
THESE MEN
GAVE THEIR LIVES
FOR THEIR COUNTRY.
ALLIN F.C.
ALFORD E.J.
APPLEYARD C.
APPLEYARD G.
APPLEYARD E.J.
BIRD F.A.
BUTLER F.W.
BOODY P.D.
BAGINGTON W.E.
BOLGER T.
BARLOW A.E.
BERRYMAN L.
COWLEY C.A.
COLE P.M.
CHENHALL H.B.
CROSS R.E.
CLAYTON C.J.
CARTER J.
CHRISTENSEN A.
DAVIS H.S.
ELLIOTT A.B.
ELLEFSEN T.E.
FOOTE E.R.V.
FILMER W.
FLEMING R.
GELLION J.F.
GOODSON G.E.
GAY E.T.
GILFOY H.
GLANFIELD W.D.
GRIMLINGTON D.
GARLAND E.L.
HEPBURN N.W.D.
HICKEY W.
JEFFS G.E.
JOHNSON C.R.H.
JOLLY S.
JONES A.
LEAR I.J.
LIVINGSTON F.
GREAT WAR
1914-1918
WE
HONOUR THE FALLEN
WORLD WAR
1939 - 1945

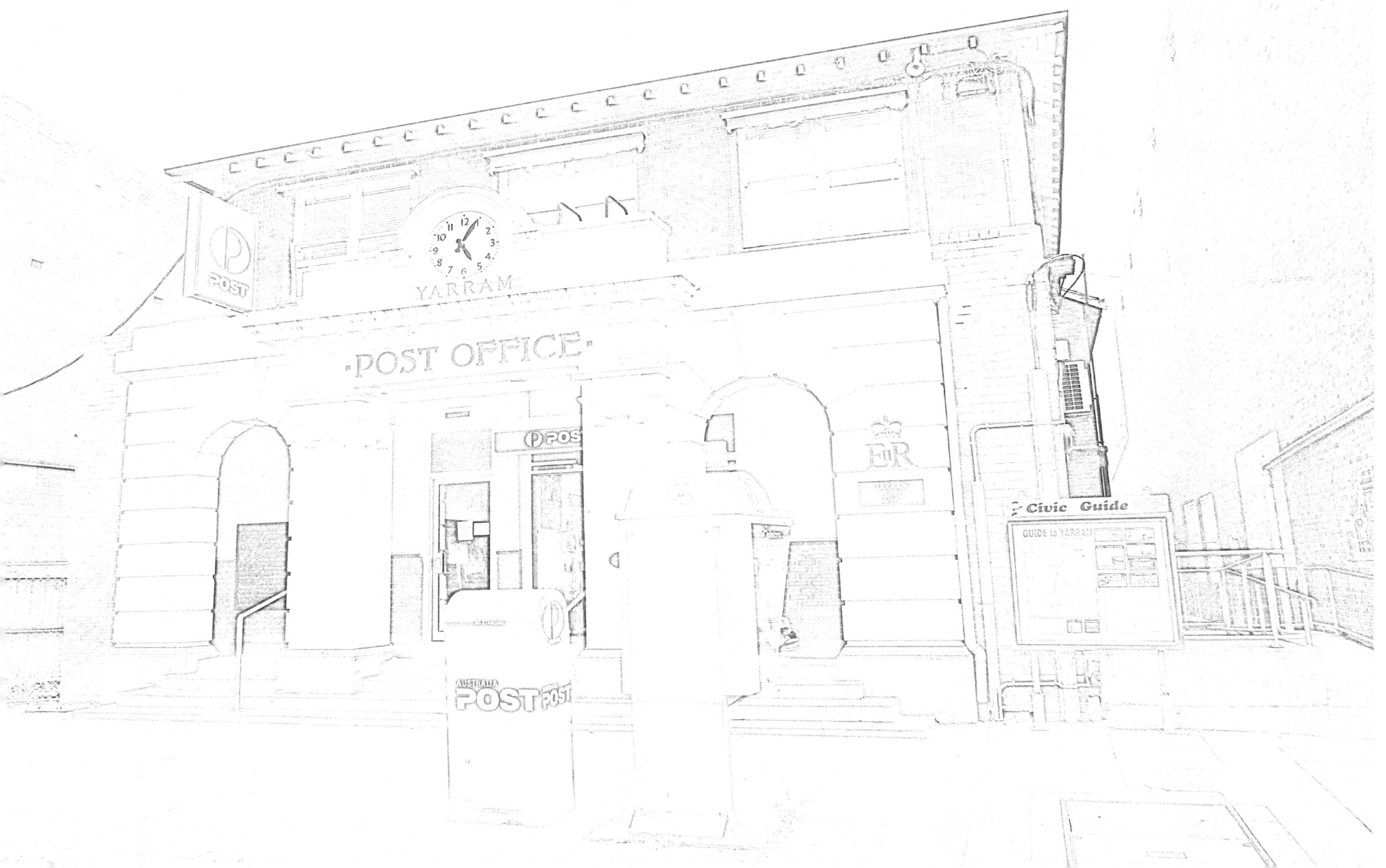
POST
YARRAM
·POST OFFICE·
POST
ER
Civic Guide
GUIDE to YARRAM
AUSTRALIA
POST
POST

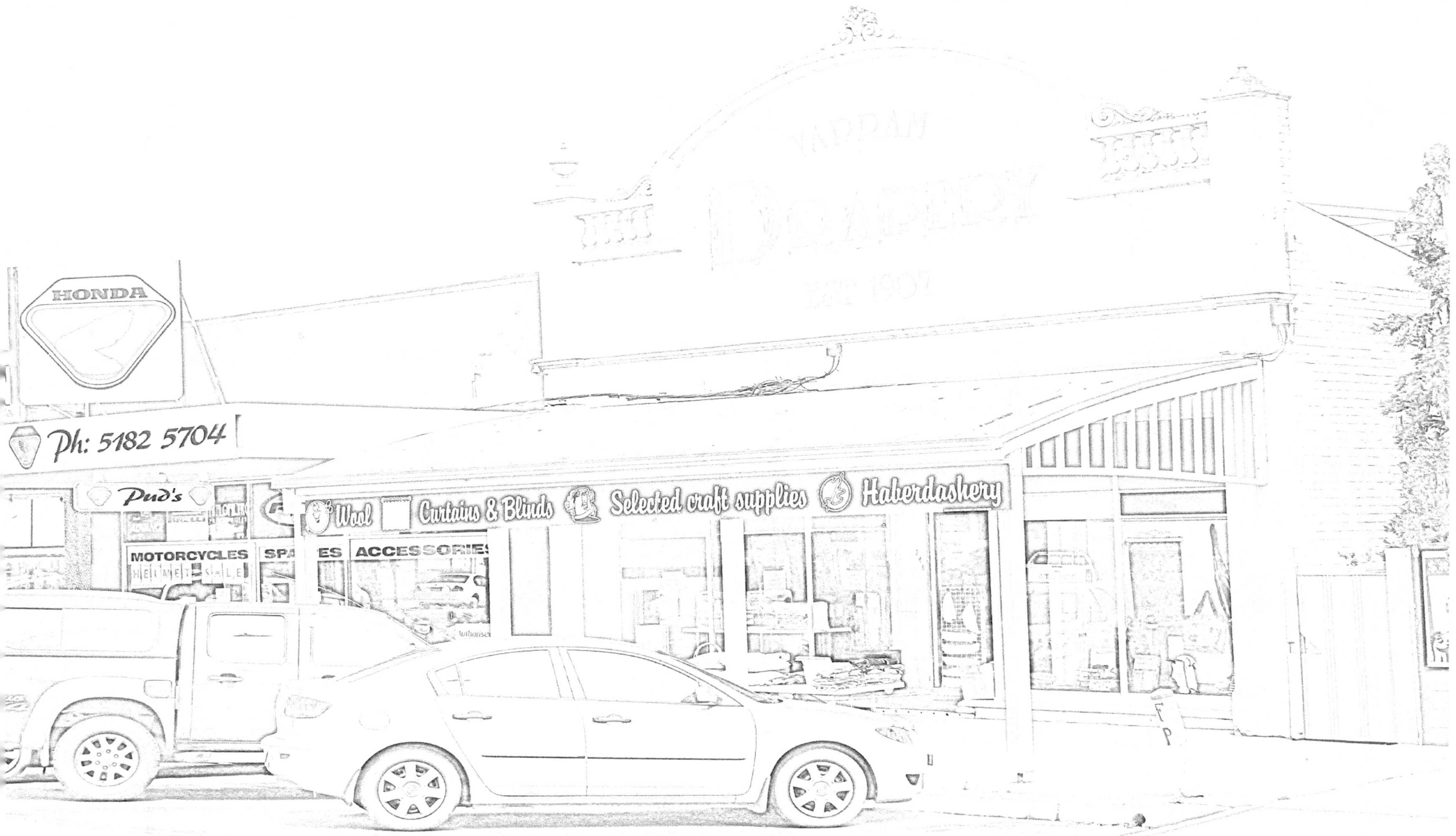

YARRAM
Est 1907
HONDA
Ph: 5182 5704
Pud's
MOTORCYCLES
ACCESSORIES
Wool
Curtains & Blinds
Selected craft supplies
Haberdashery

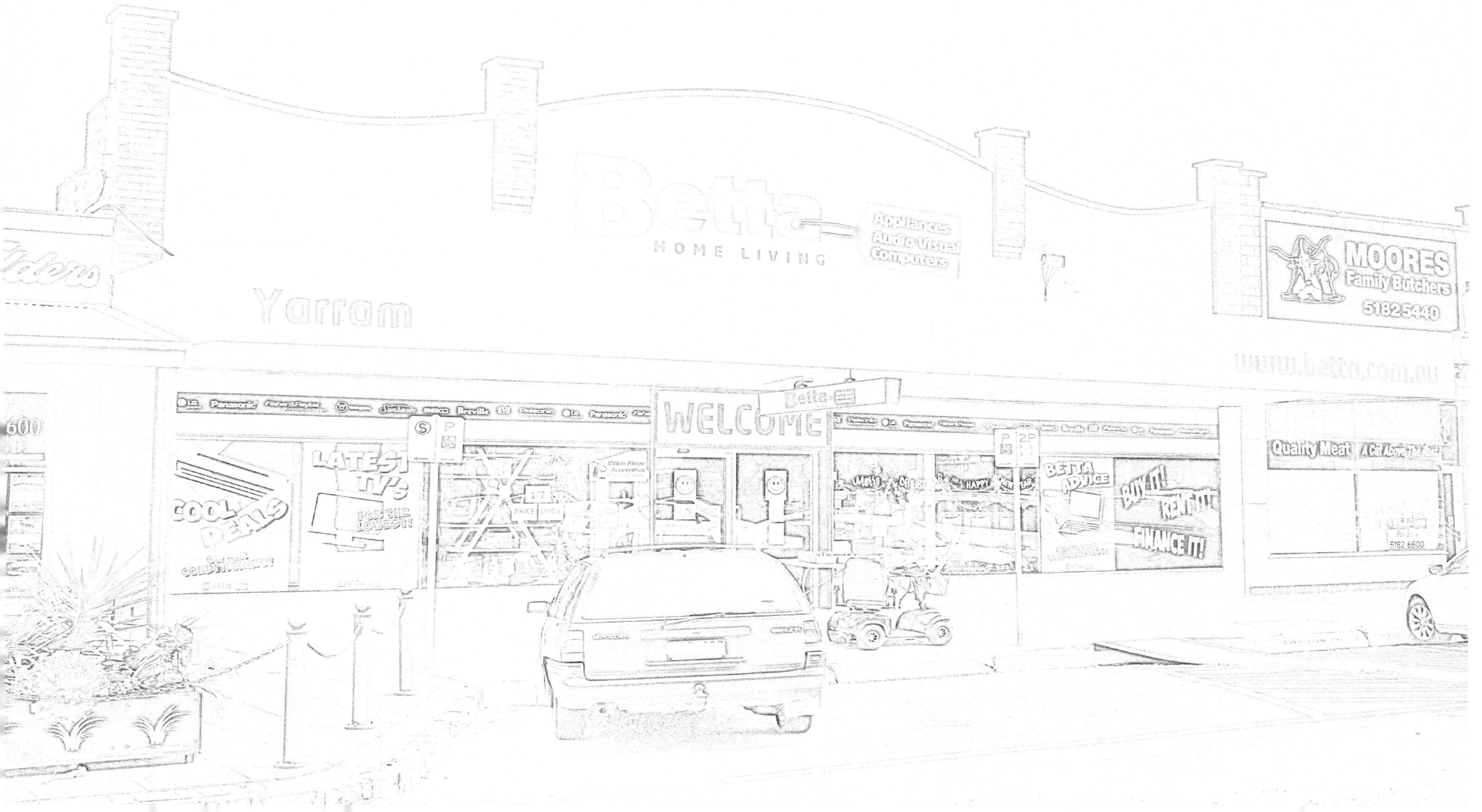
Betta
HOME LIVING
Appliances
Audio Visual
Computers
Yarram
MOORES
Family Butchers
5182 5440
www.betta.com.au
WELCOME
Quality Meat
COOL DEALS
LATEST TV'S
FOR THE LOWEST!
BETTA ADVICE
BUY IT!
RENT IT!
FINANCE IT!
5182 6600

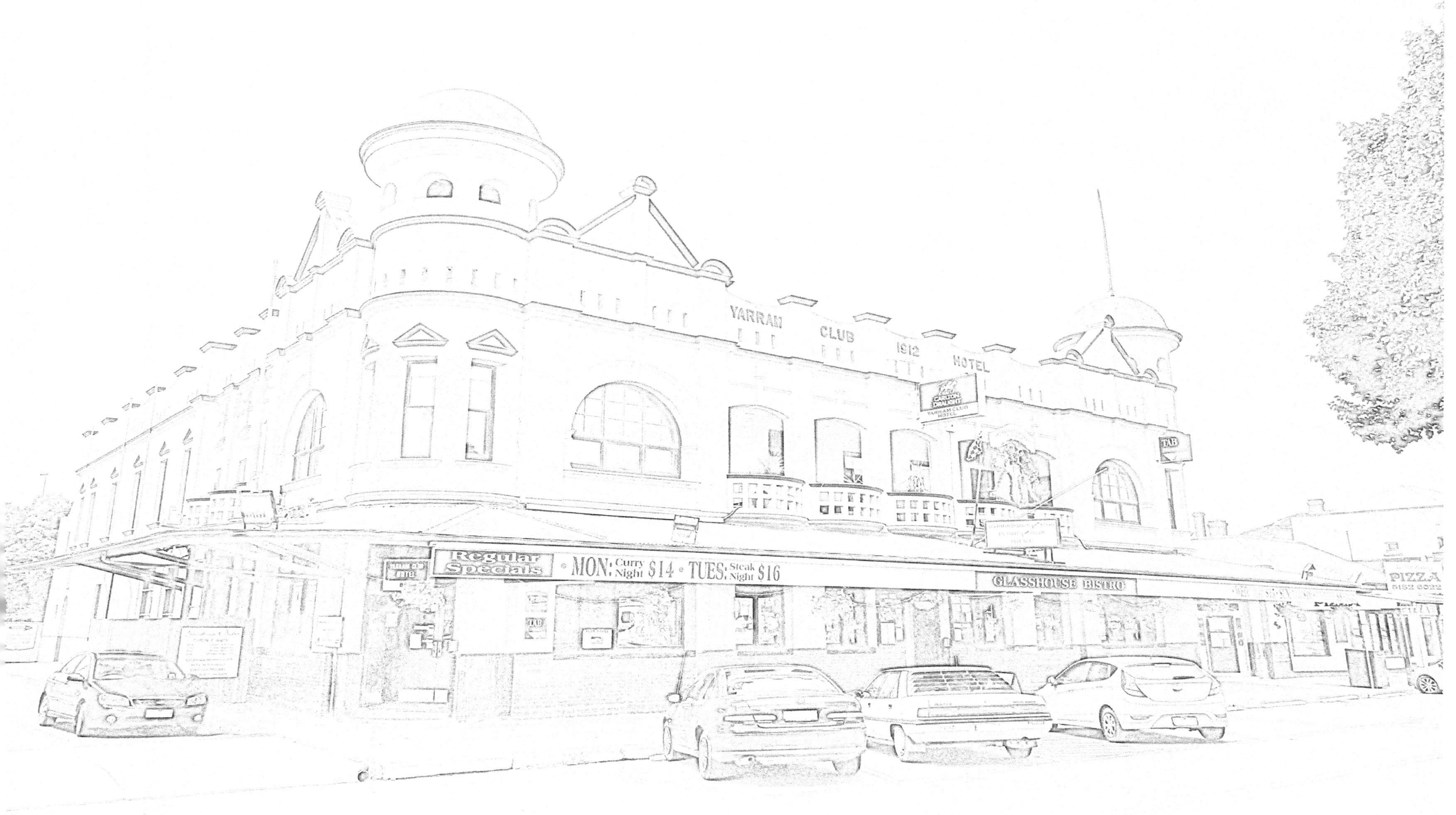
YARRAM CLUB 1912 HOTEL
Regular Specials
MON: Curry Night $14 • TUES: Steak Night $16
GLASSHOUSE BISTRO
TAB
PIZZA

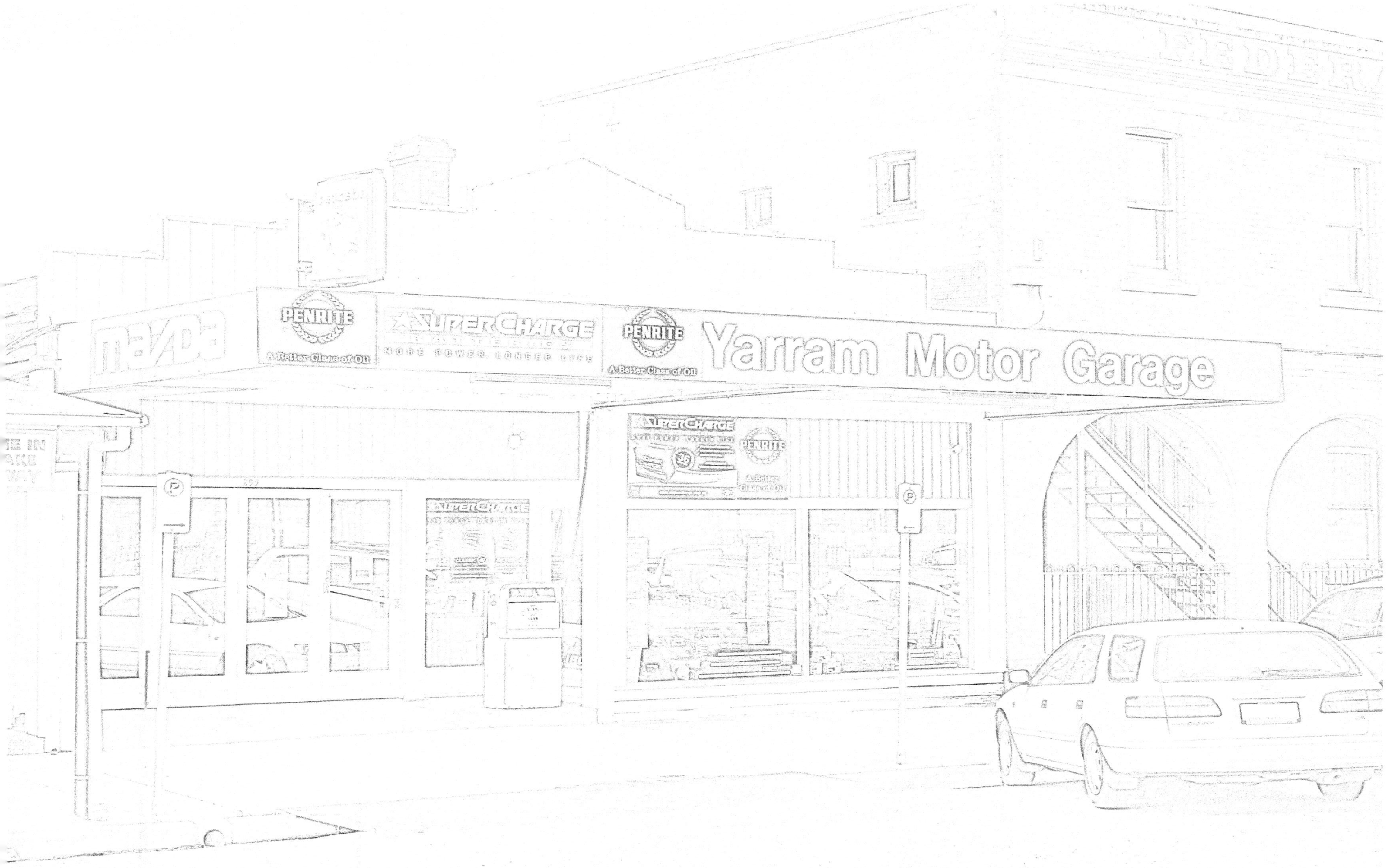
Yarram Motor Garage
PENRITE
A Better Class of Oil
SUPERCHARGE
MORE POWER. LONGER LIFE
PENRITE
A Better Class of Oil
mazda
P
P

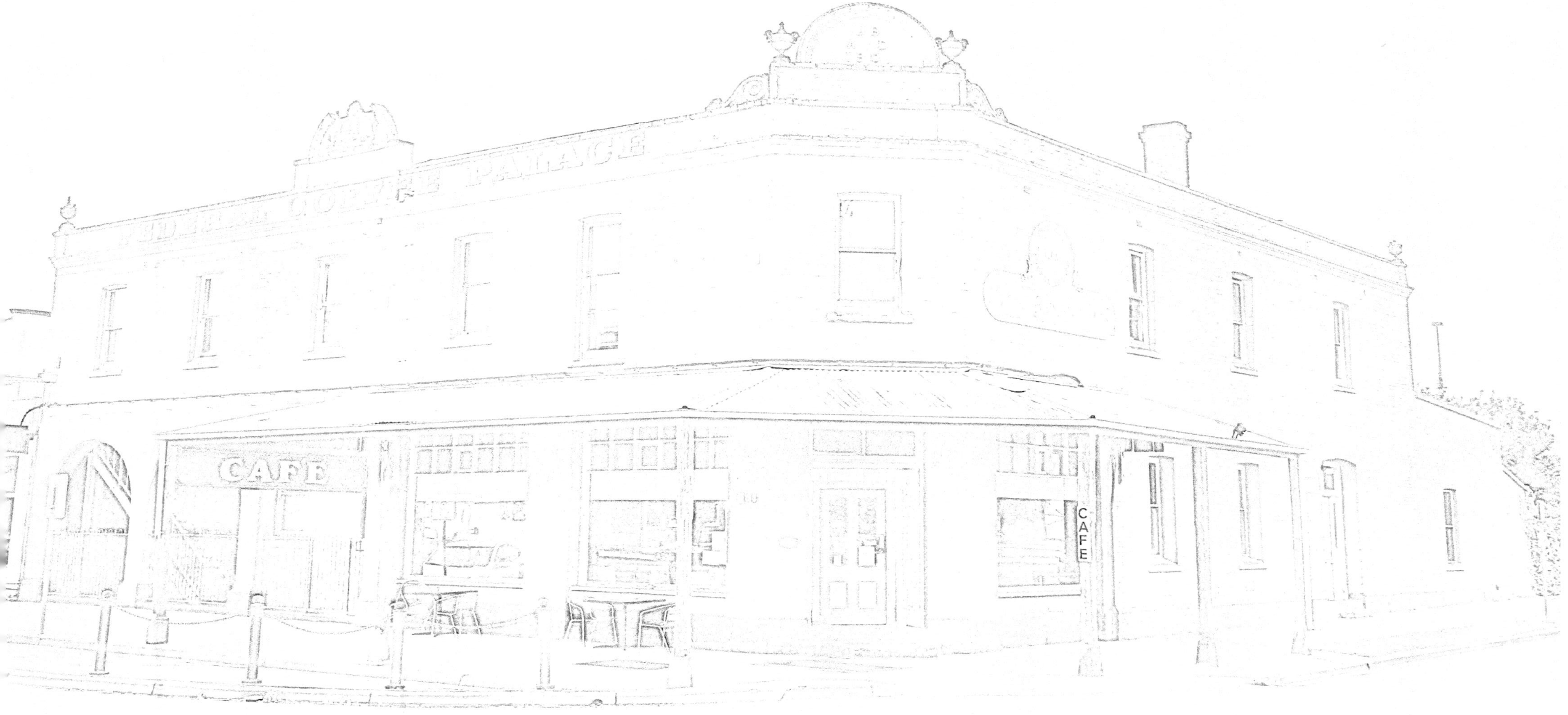
PALACE
CAFE
CAFE

GRANT ST
community

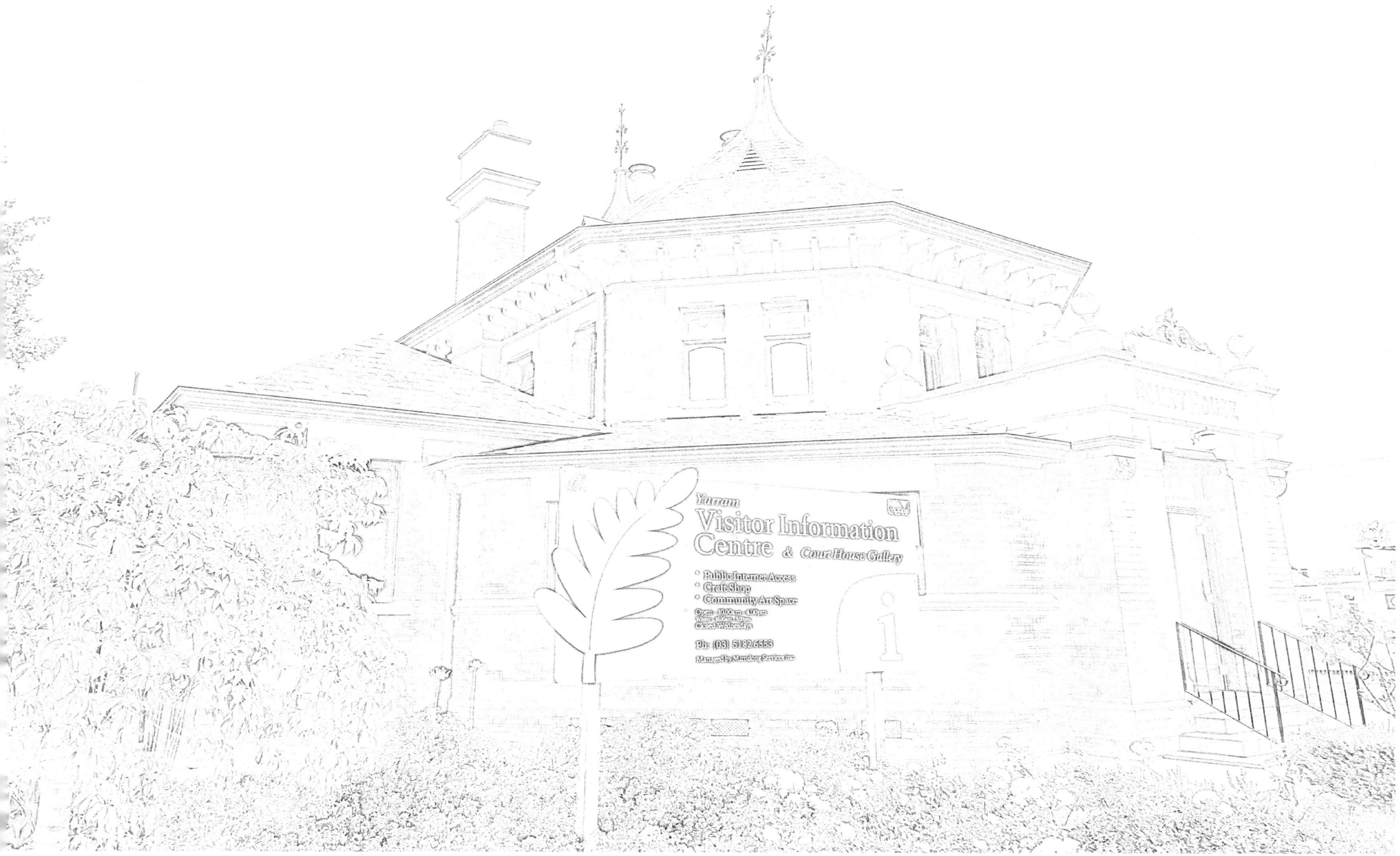
Yarram
Visitor Information
Centre & Court House Gallery
Public Internet Access
Craft Shop
Community Art Space
Ph: (03) 5182 6553

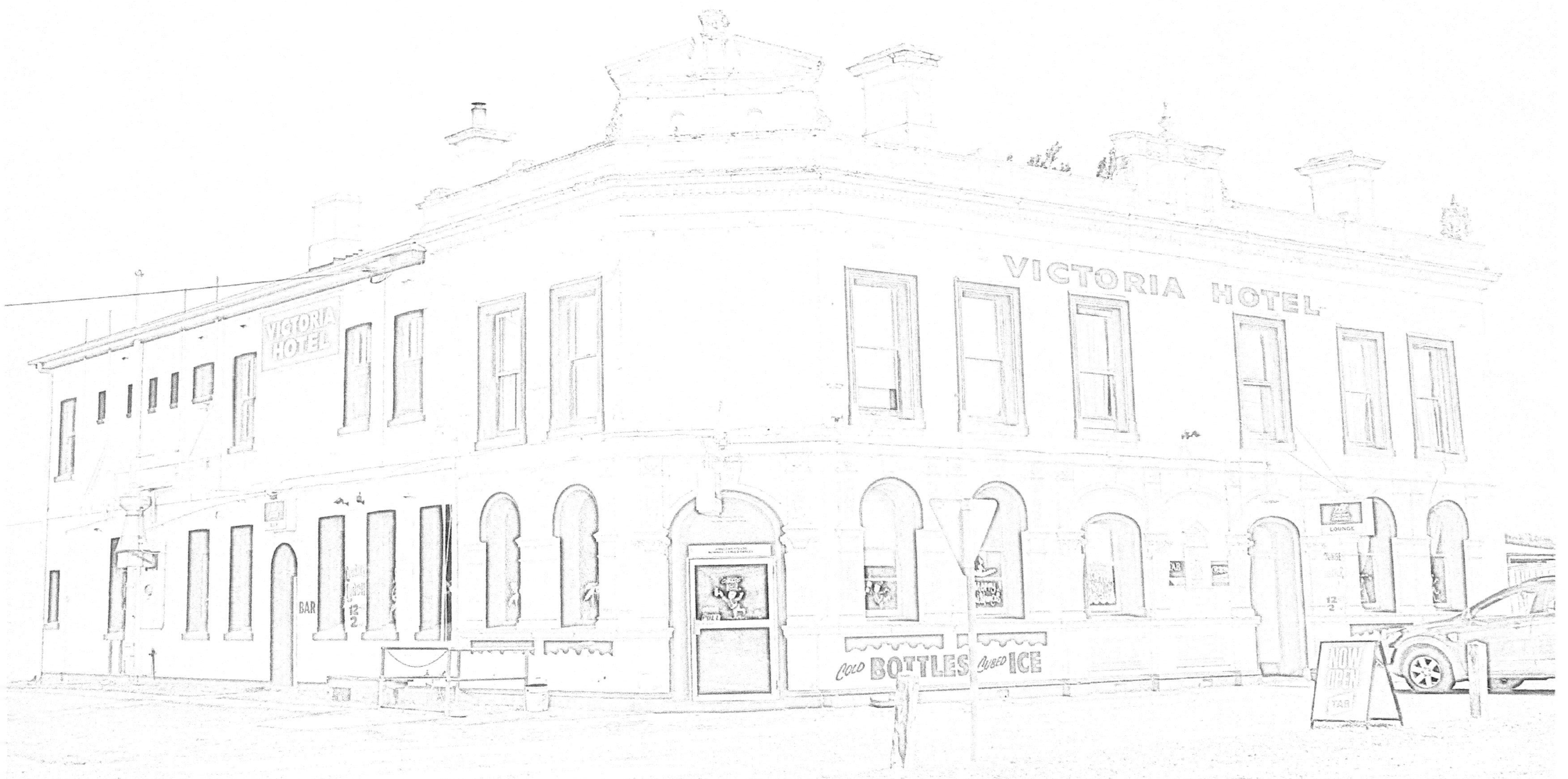
VICTORIA HOTEL
VICTORIA HOTEL
BAR
LOUNGE
COLD BOTTLES CUBED ICE
NOW OPEN
TAB

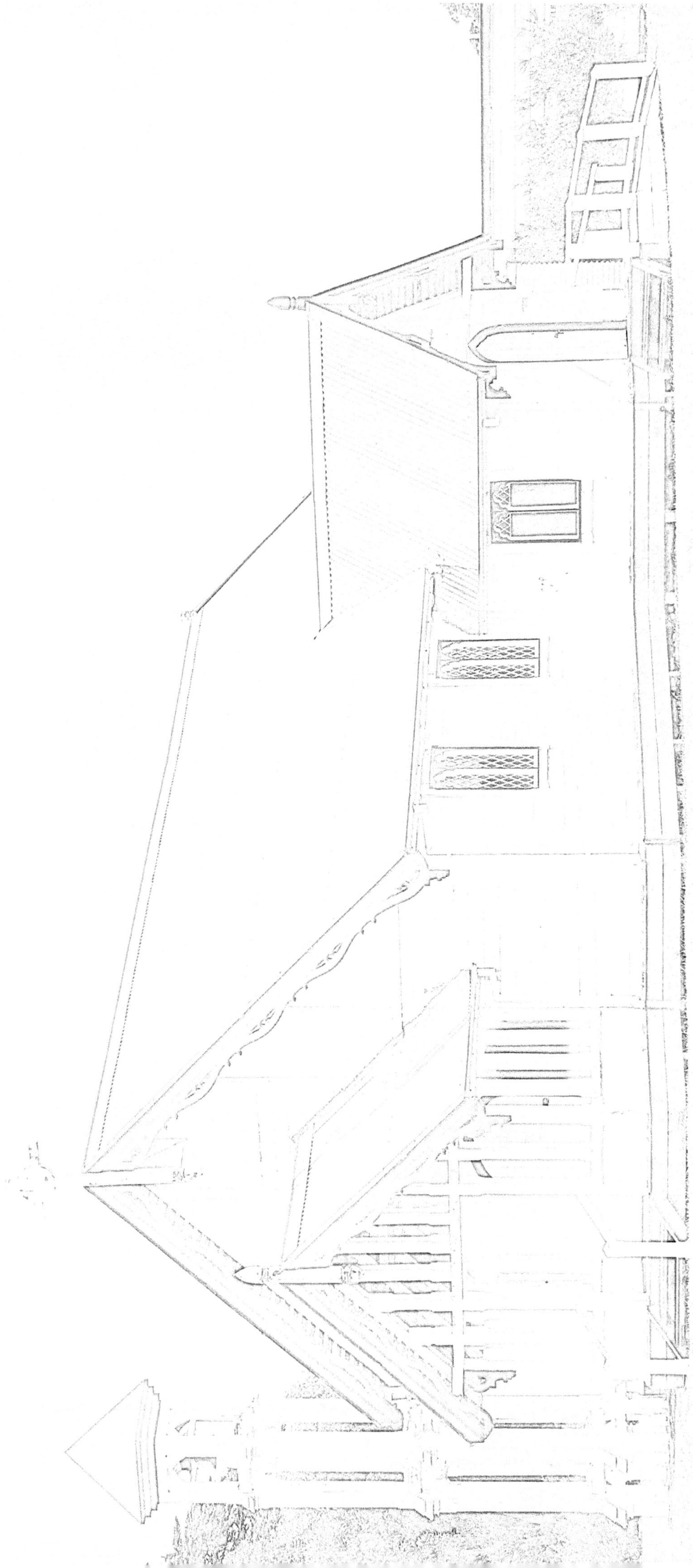

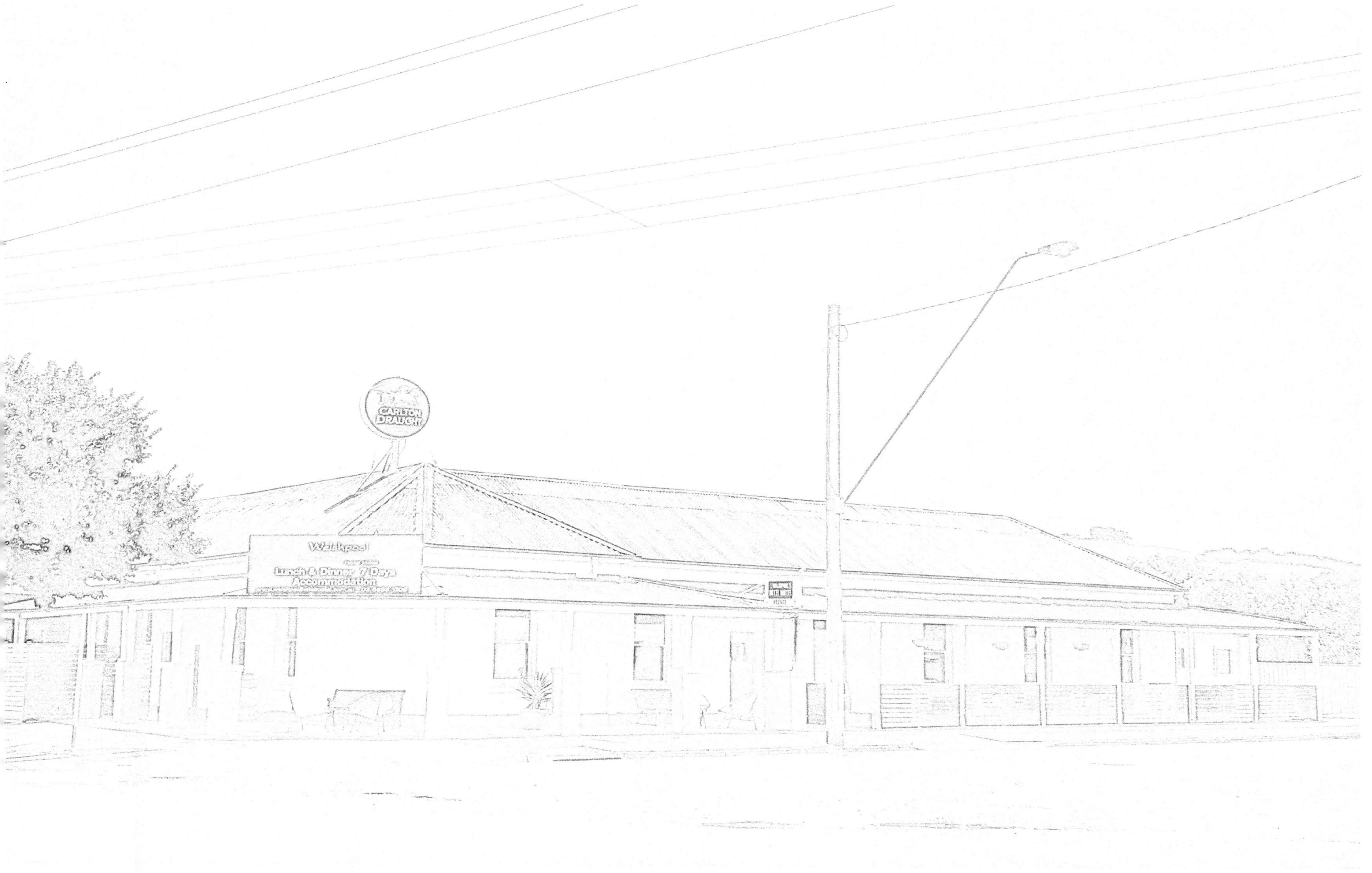
CARLTON DRAUGHT
Lunch & Dinner 7 Days
Accommodation

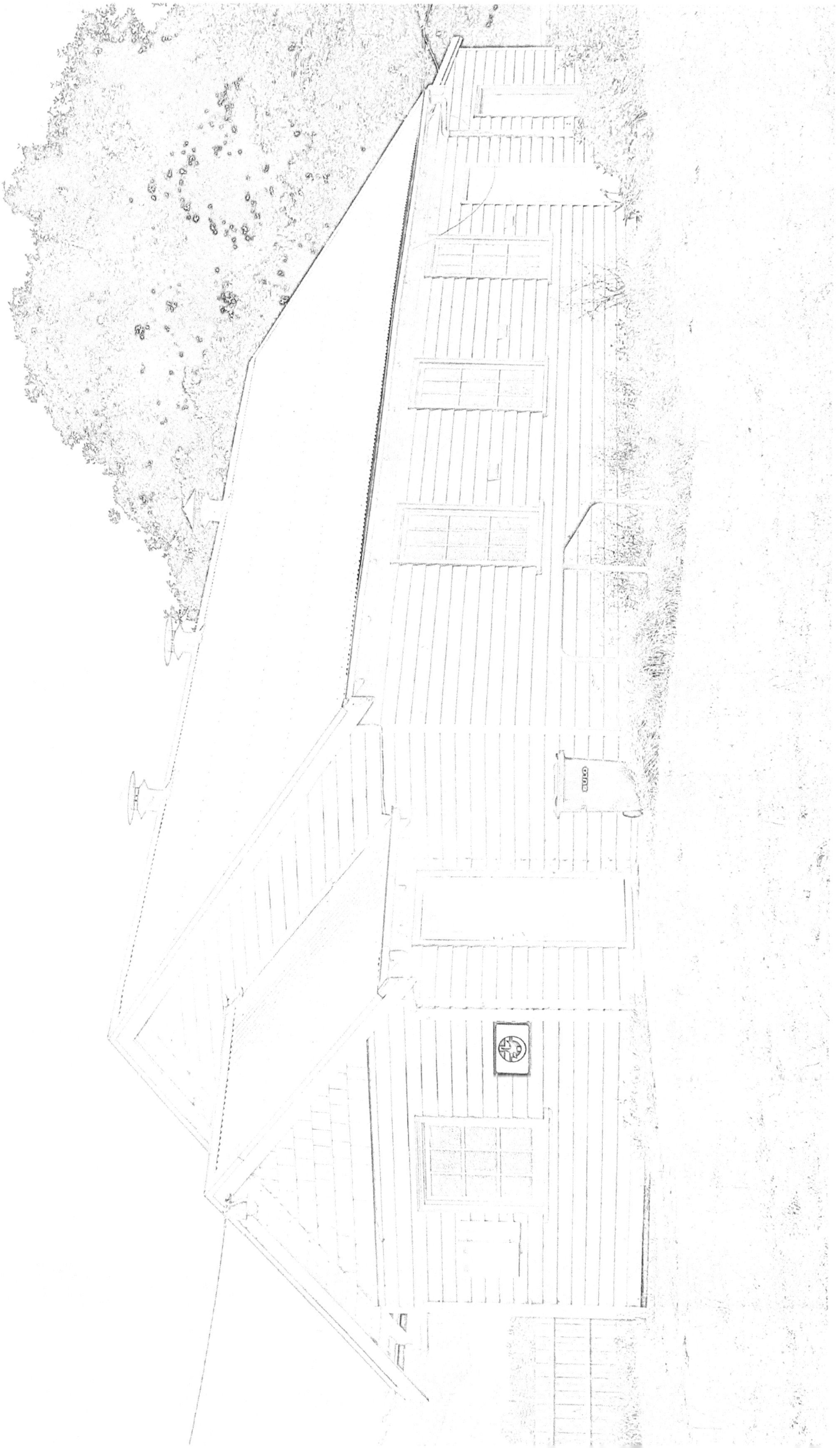

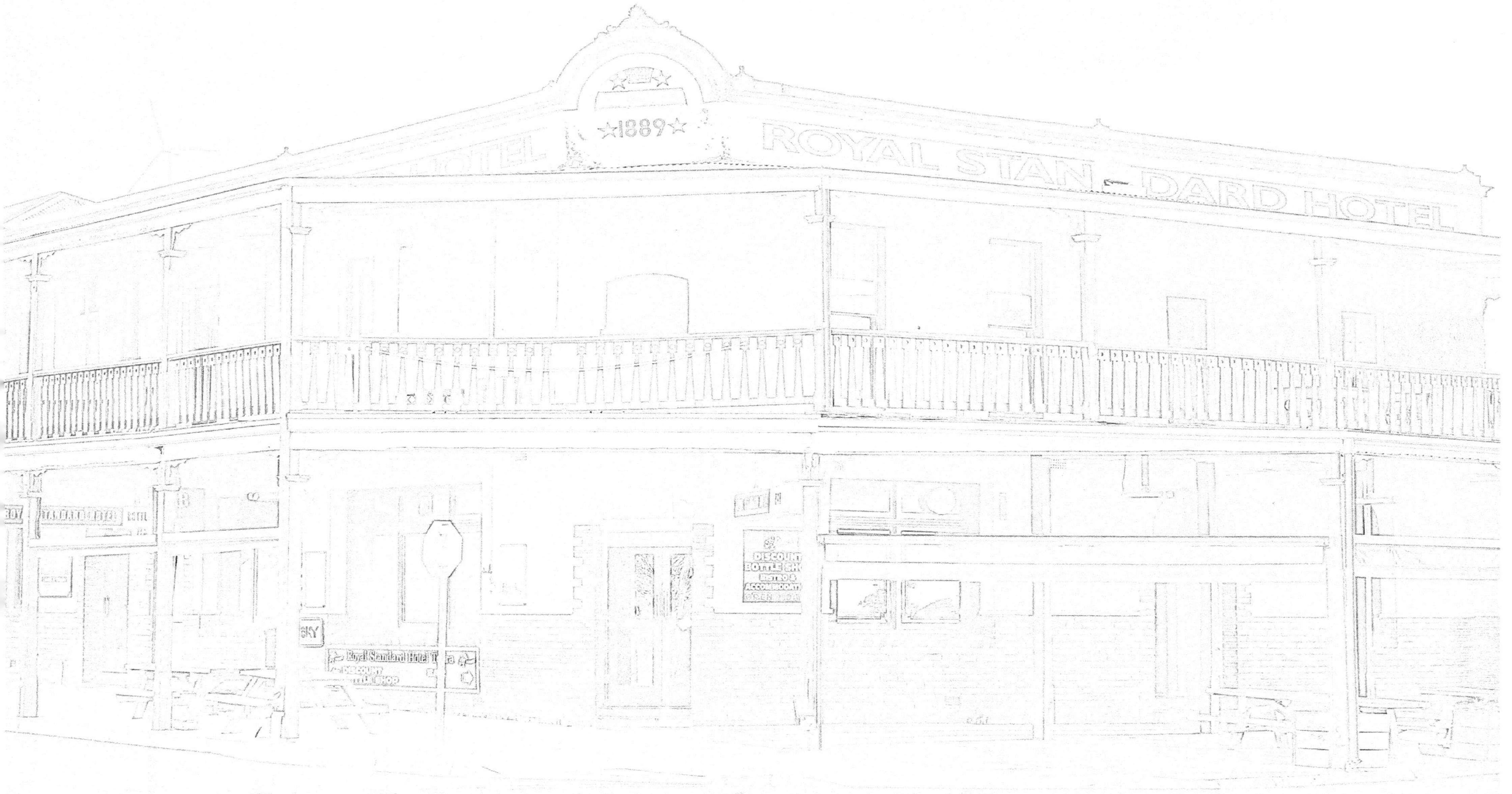
HOTEL
1889
ROYAL STANDARD HOTEL
DISCOUNT
BOTTLE SH
Royal Standard Hotel

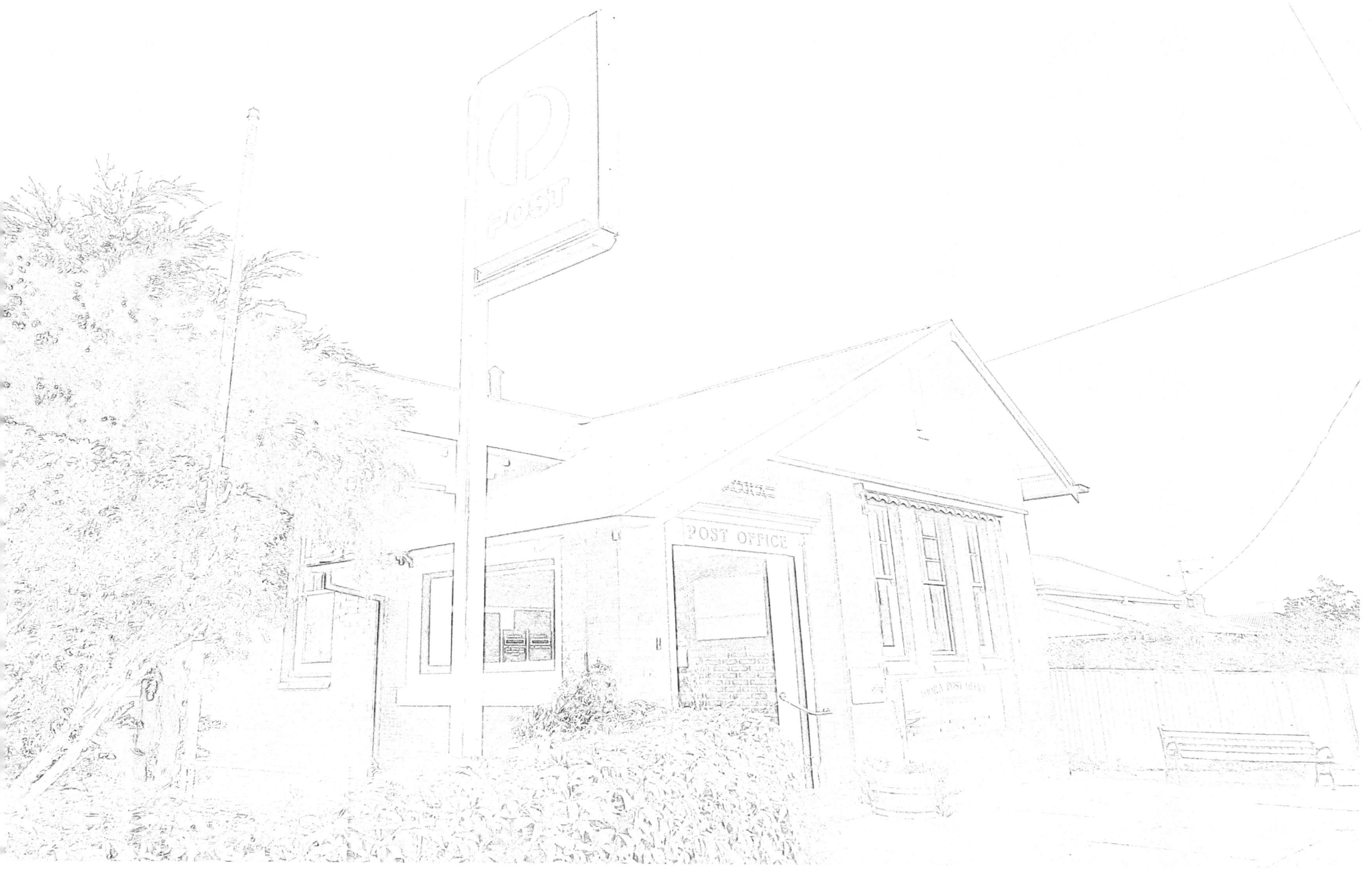
POST
POST OFFICE

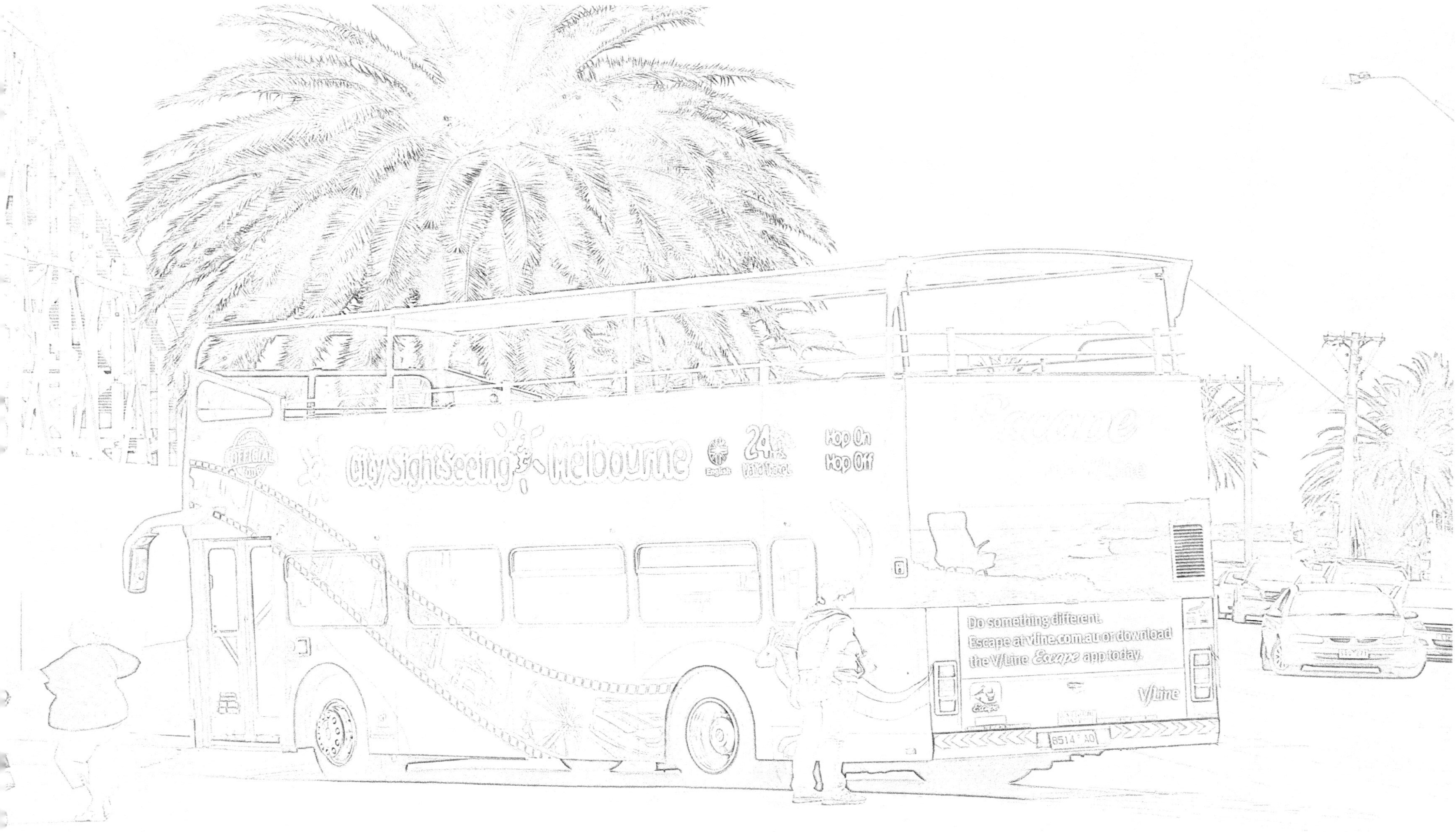
City SightSeeing Melbourne
Hop On
Hop Off
Do something different.
Escape at vline.com.au or download
the V/Line Escape app today.
V/Line

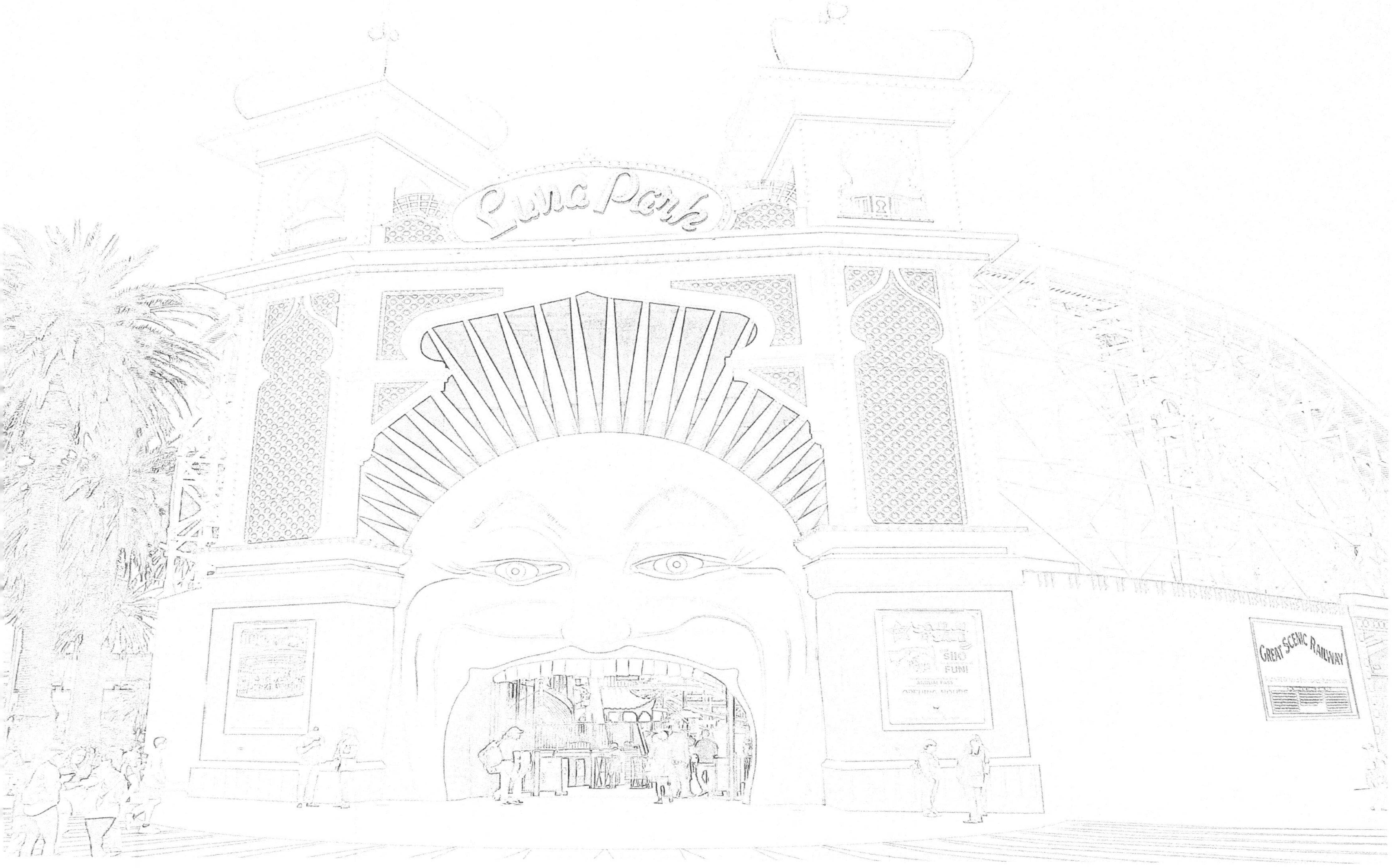
Luna Park
GREAT SCENIC RAILWAY

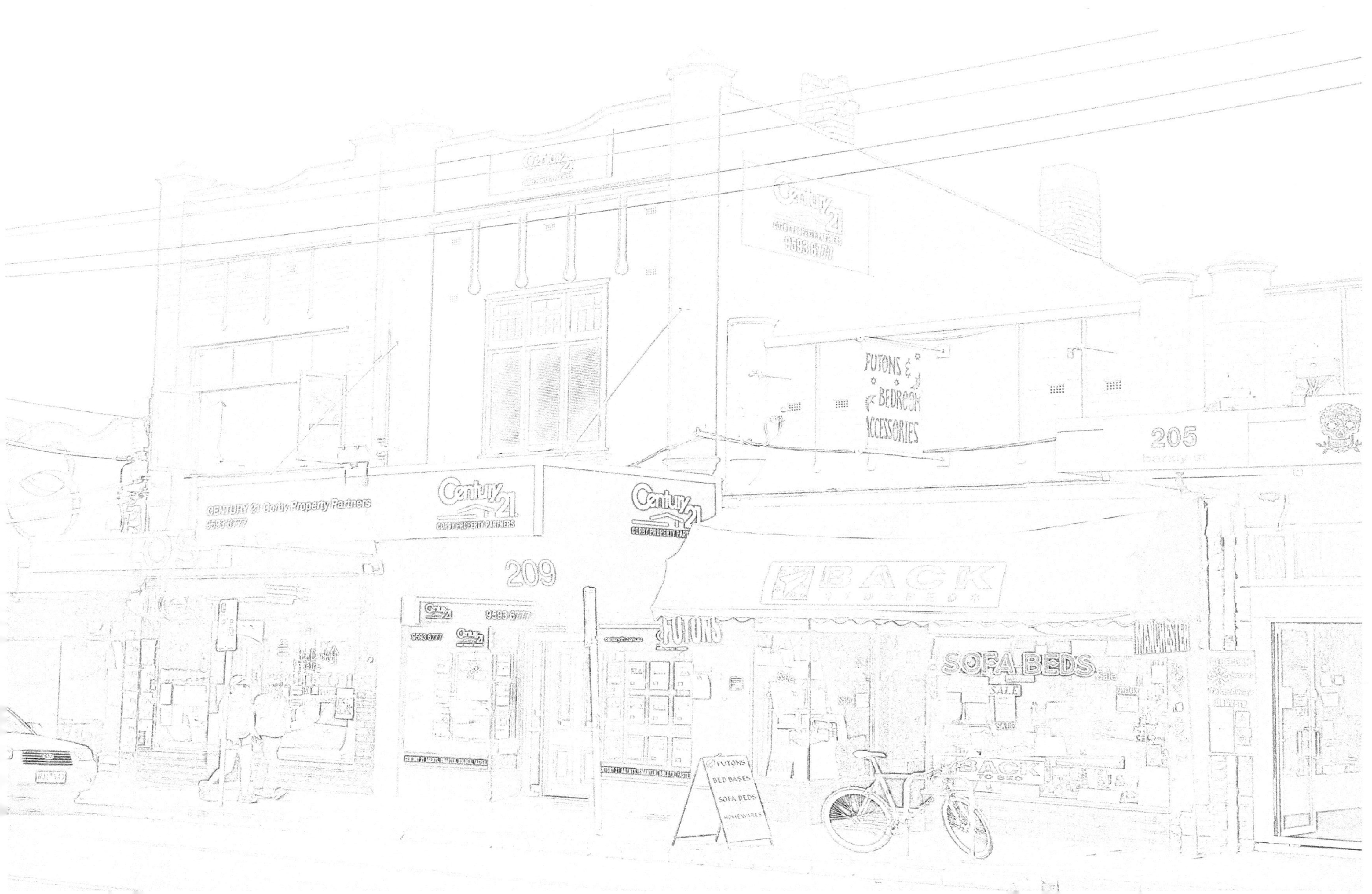
Century 21
Century 21
CORBY PROPERTY PARTNERS
CENTURY 21 Corby Property Partners
9593 6777
209
9593 6777
FUTONS
BACK TO BED
FUTONS &
BEDROOM
ACCESSORIES
205
barkly st
SOFA BEDS
SALE
BACK TO BED
FUTONS
BED BASES
SOFA BEDS
HOMEWARES

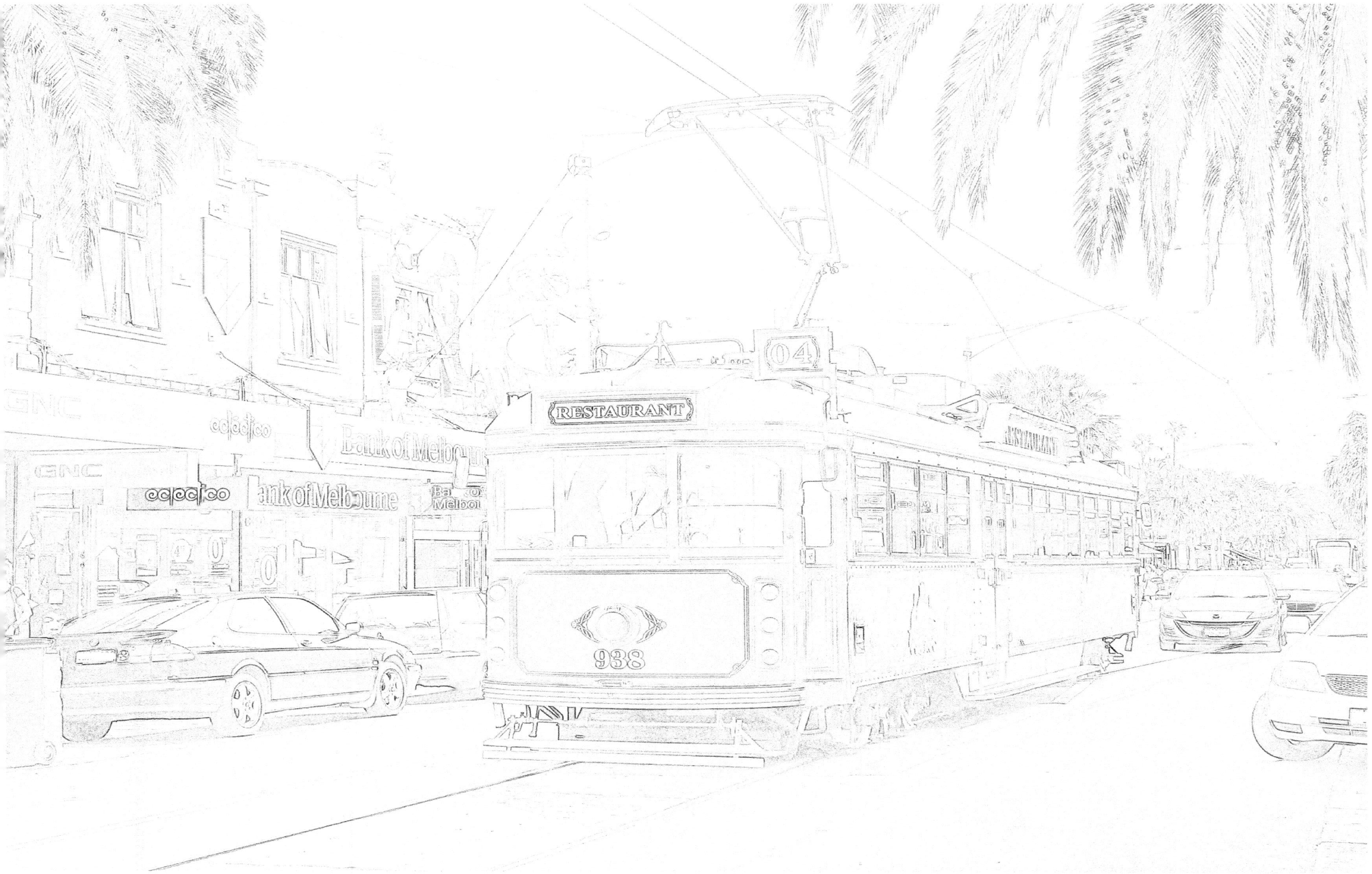
RESTAURANT
04
938
GNC
eclectico
Bank of Melbourne

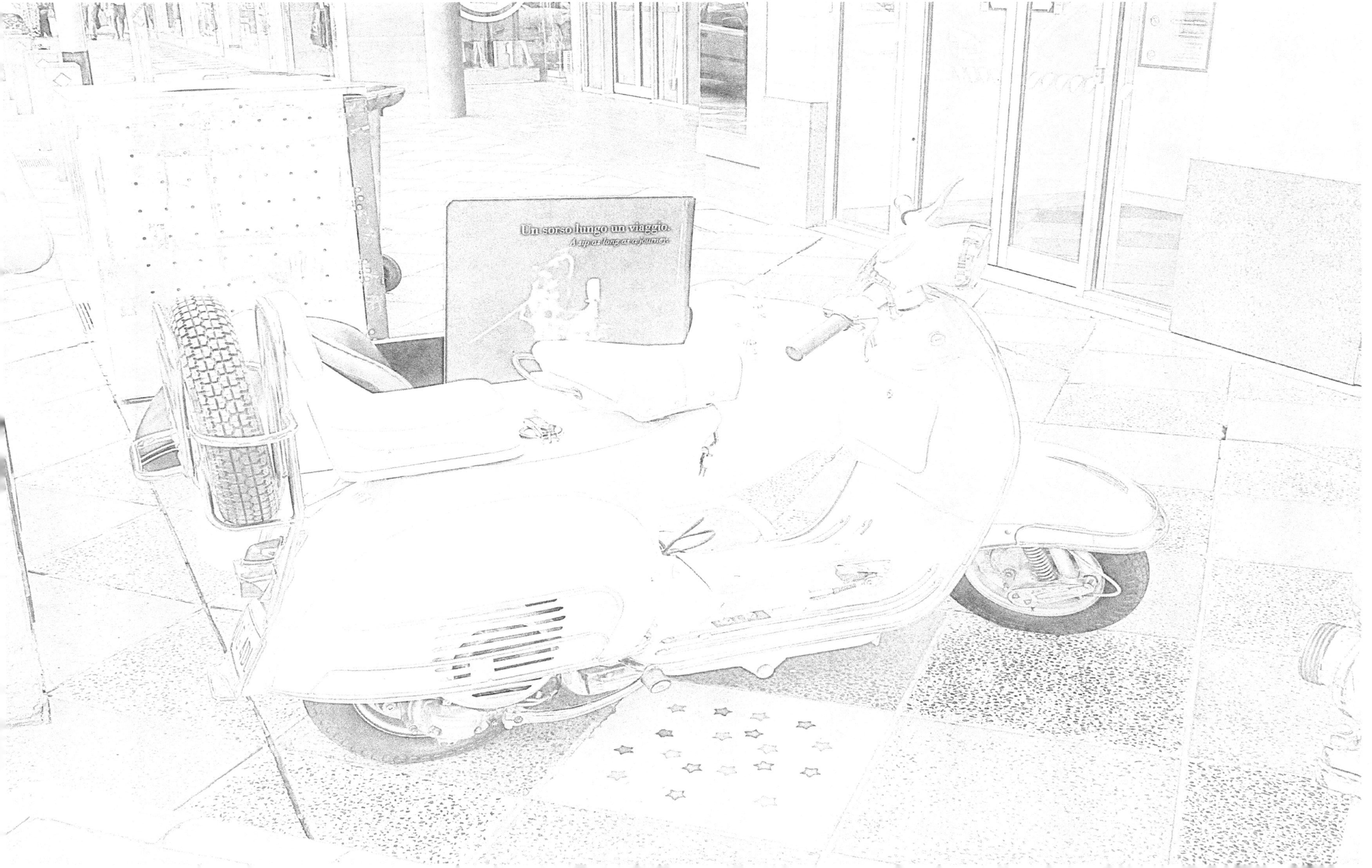
Un sorso lungo un viaggio.
A sip as long as a journey.

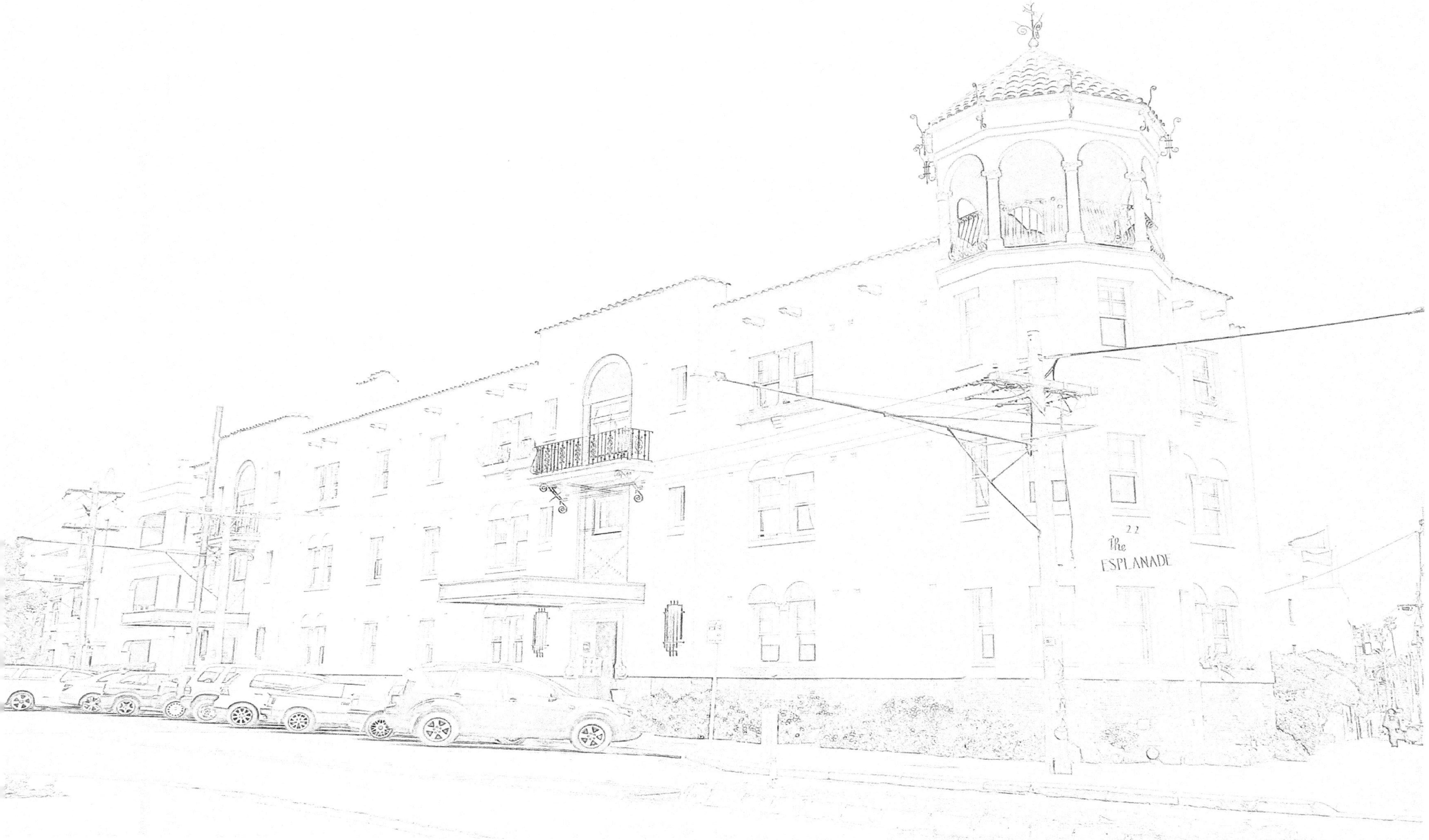
22
The
ESPLANADE

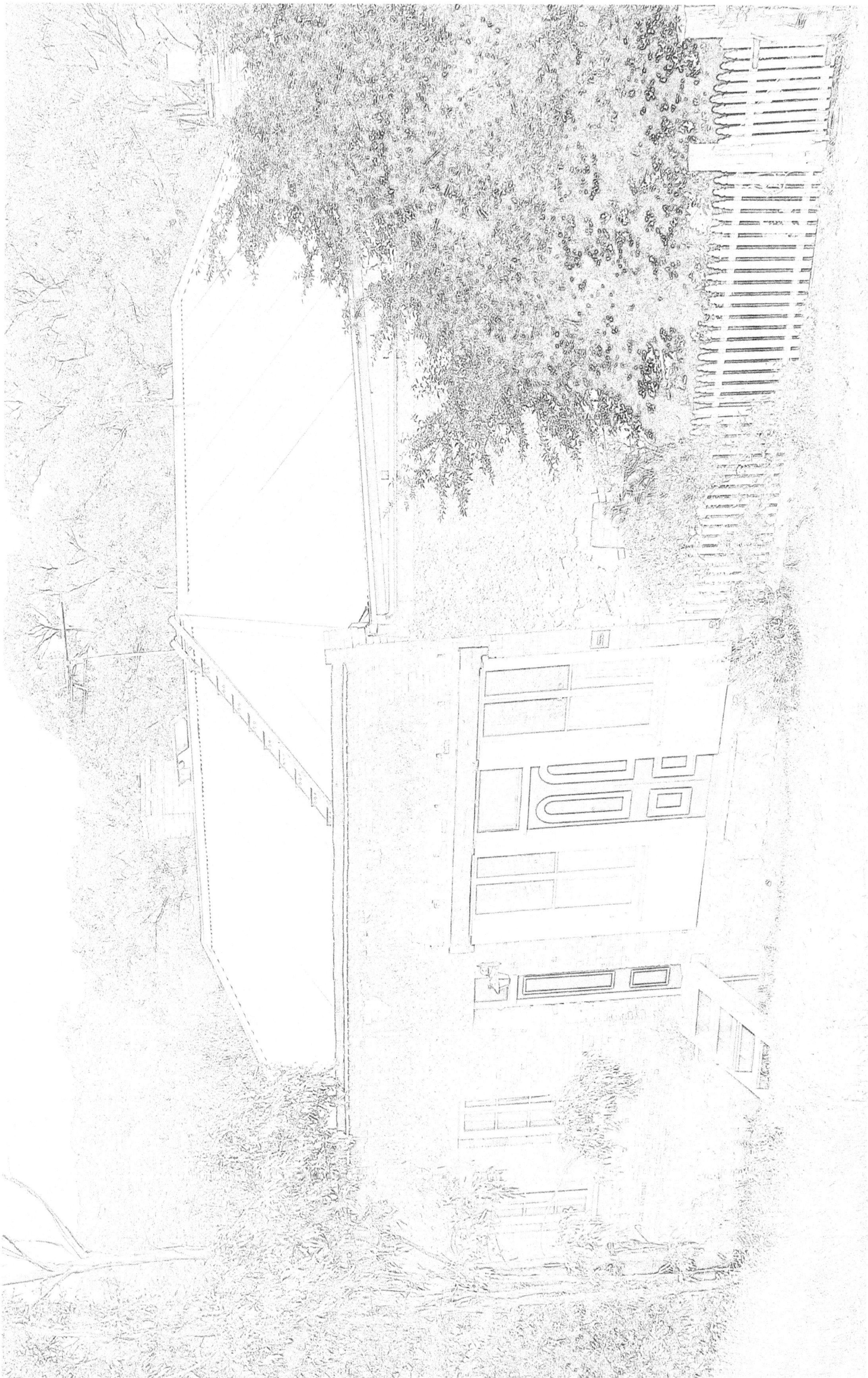

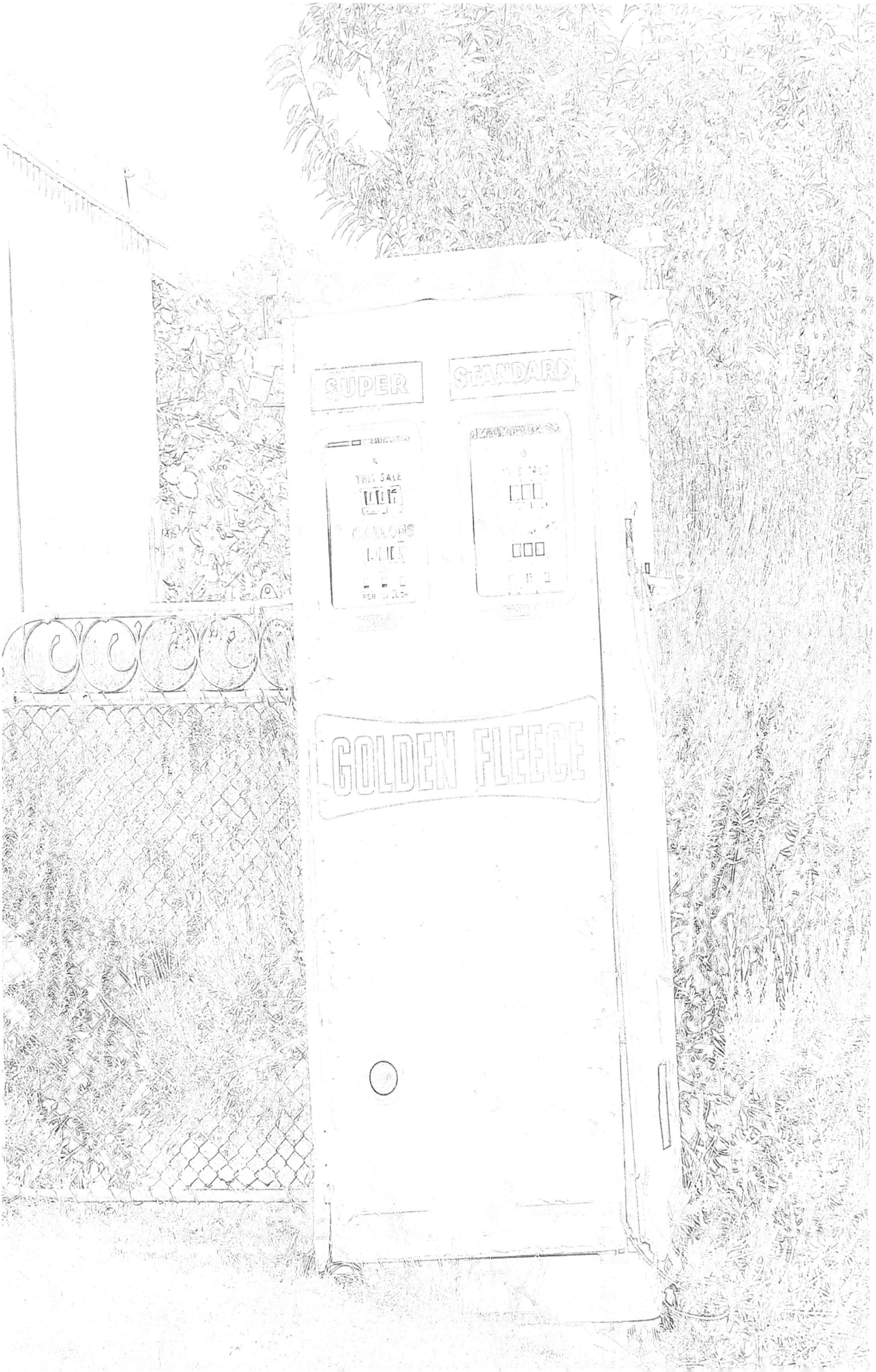
SUPER
STANDARD
THIS SALE
GALLONS
GOLDEN FLEECE

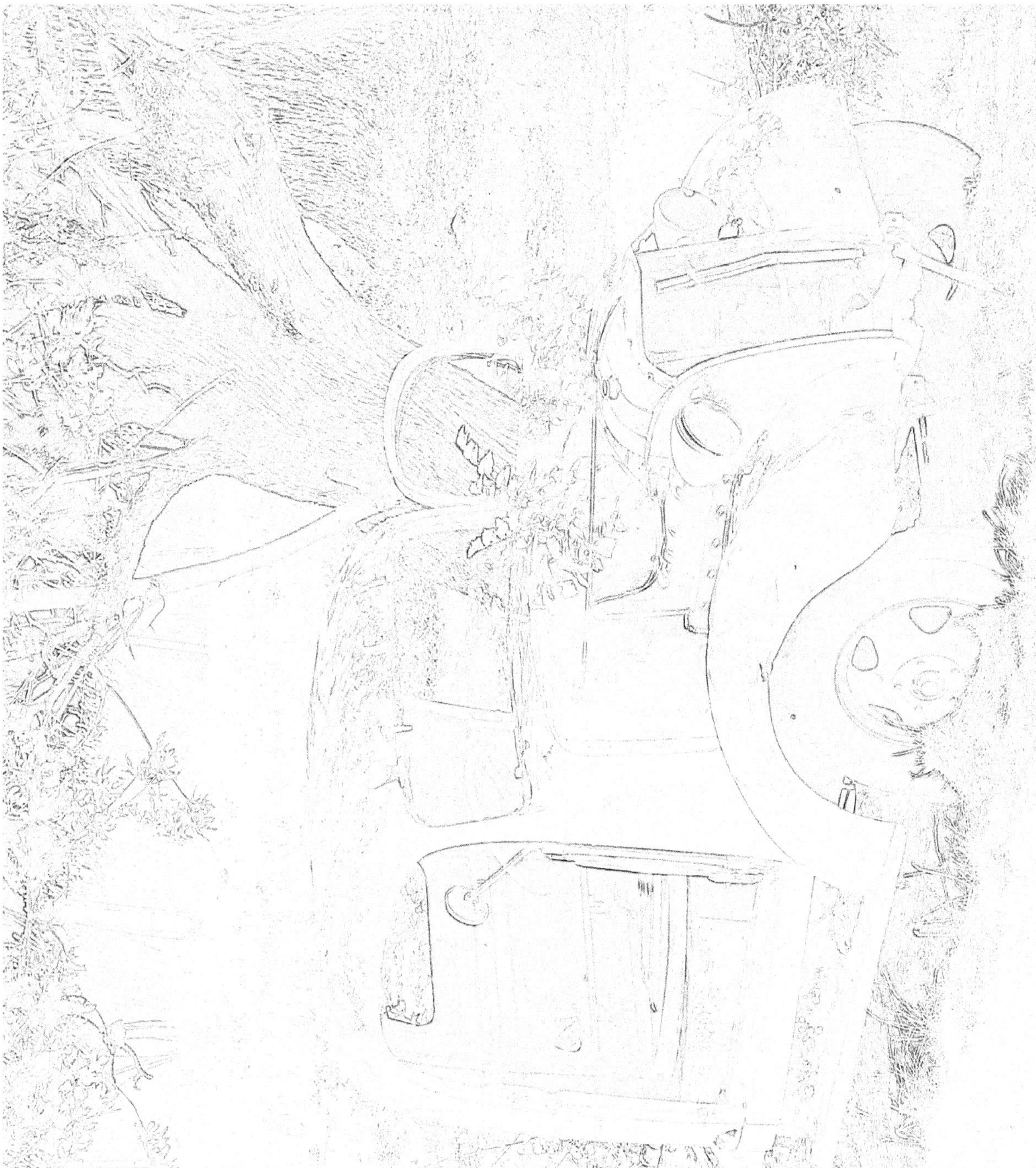

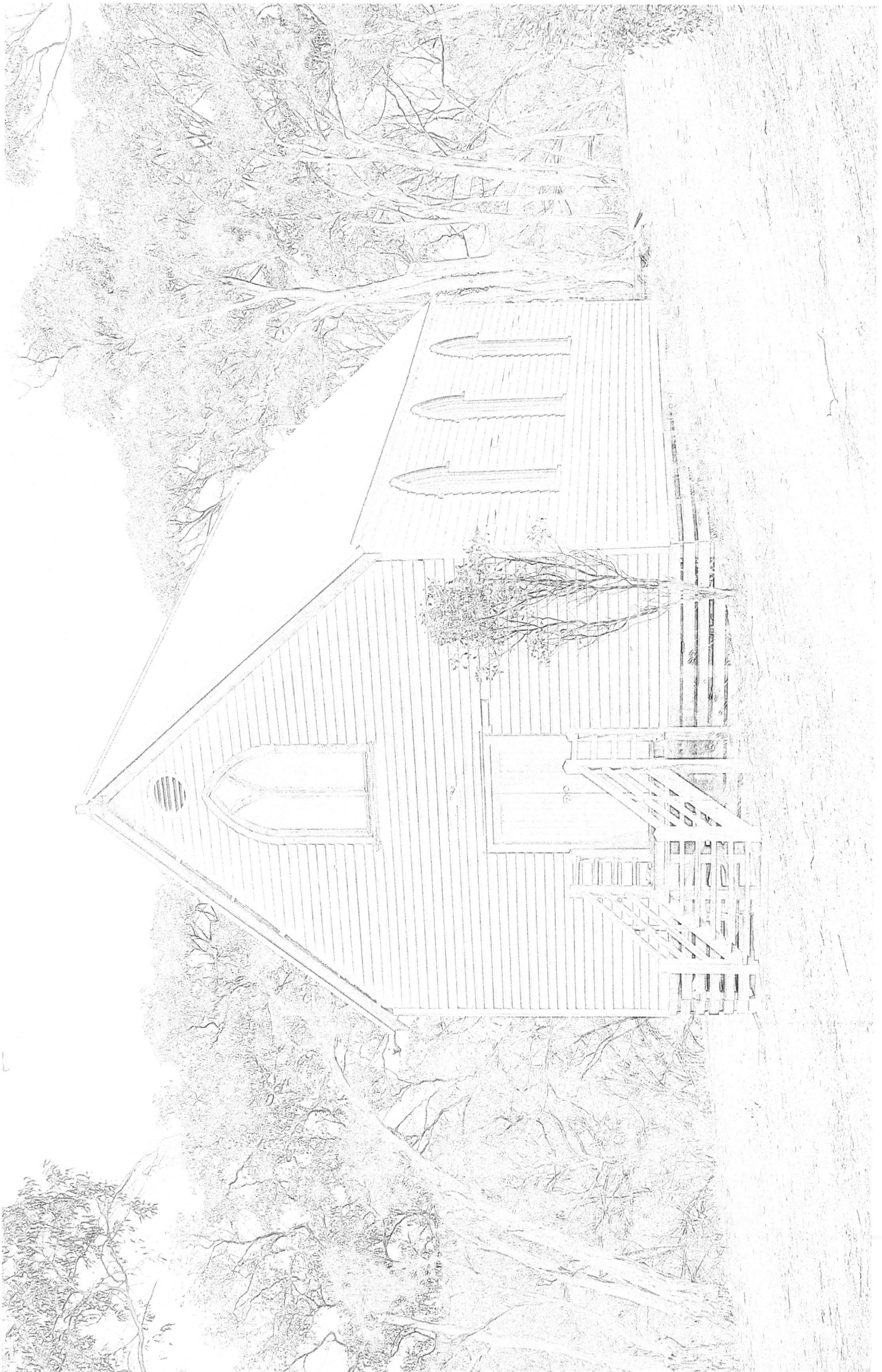

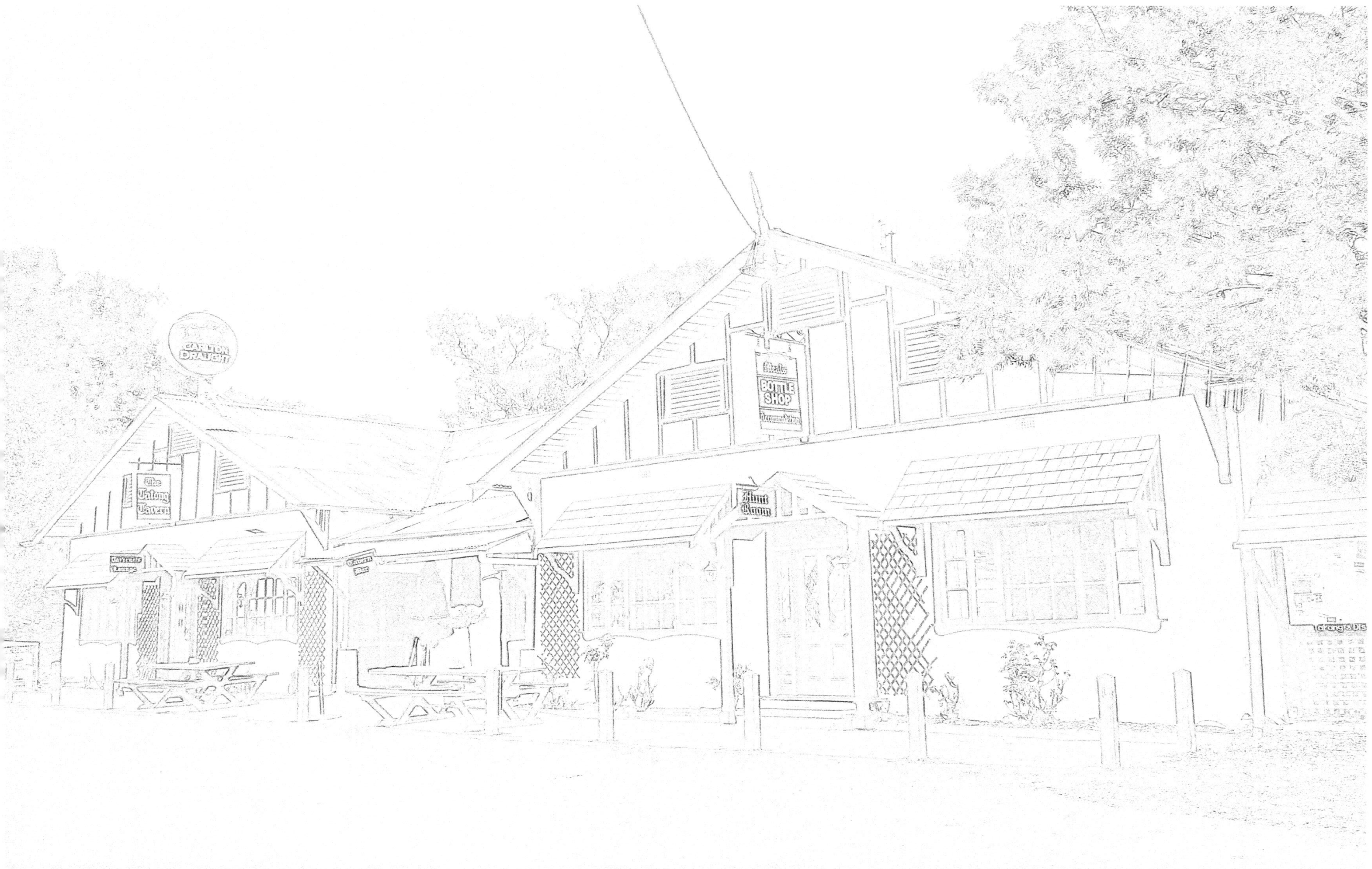
CARLTON DRAUGHT
The Tatong Tavern
Meals
BOTTLE SHOP
Hunt Room

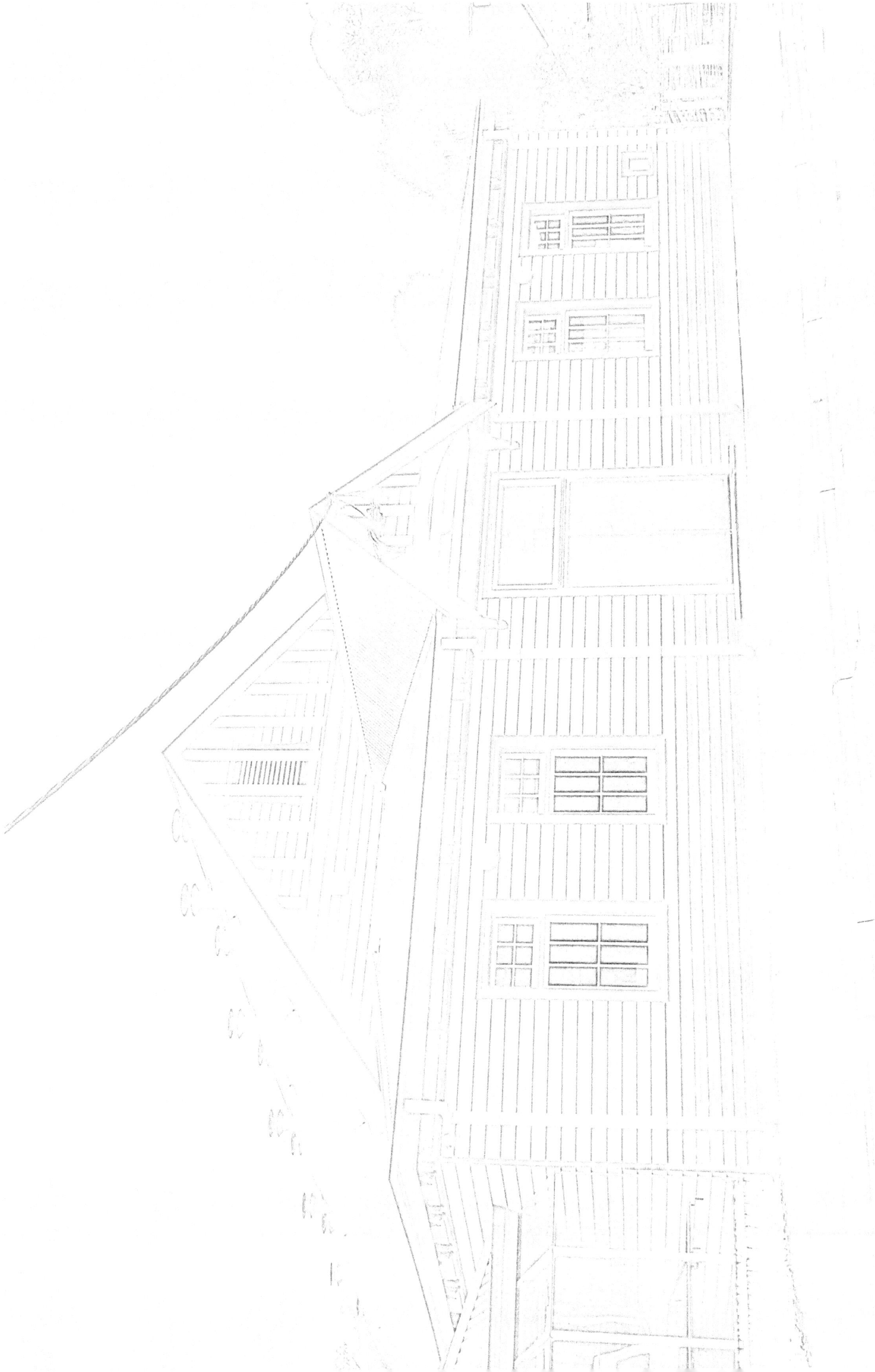

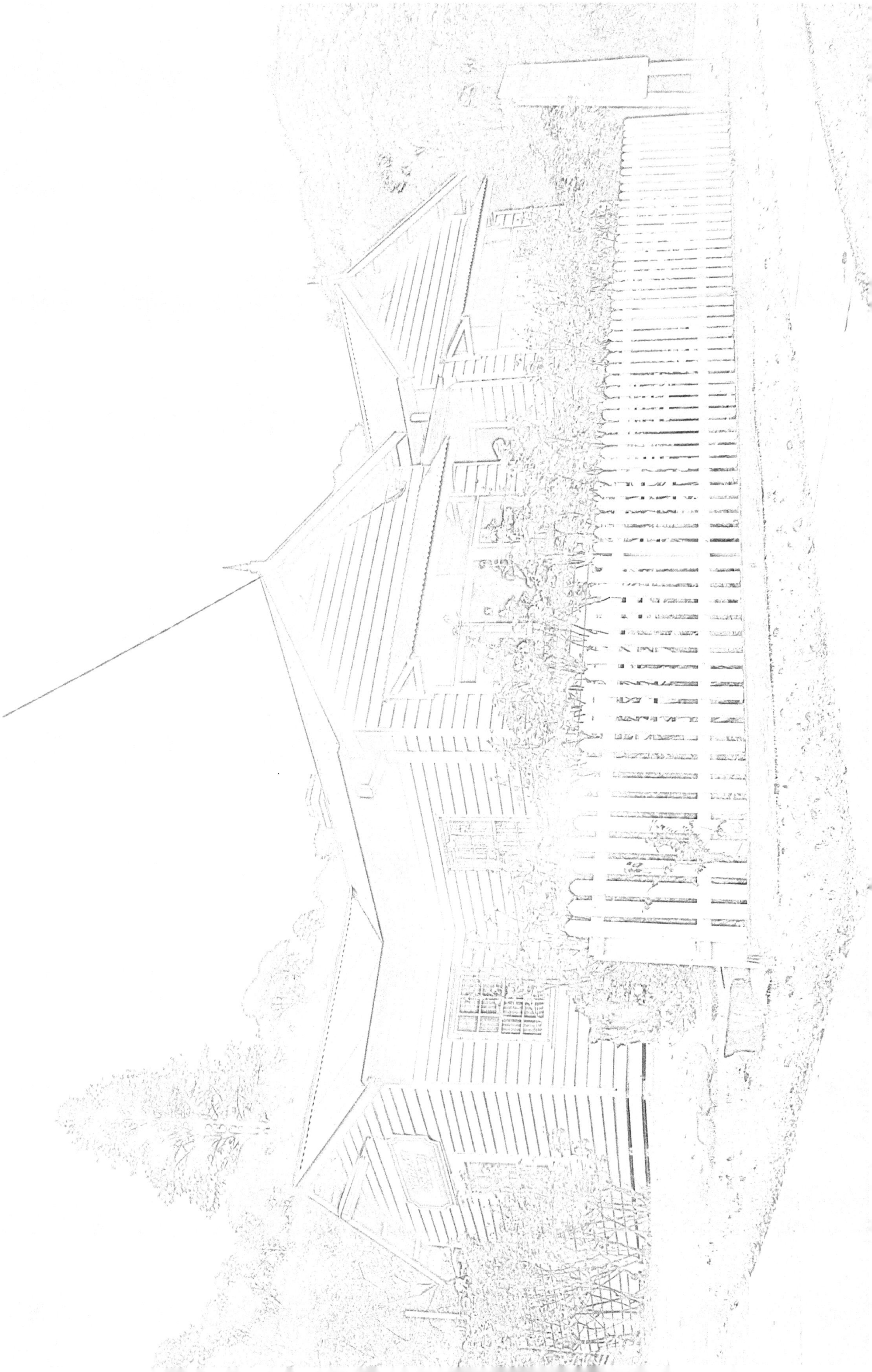

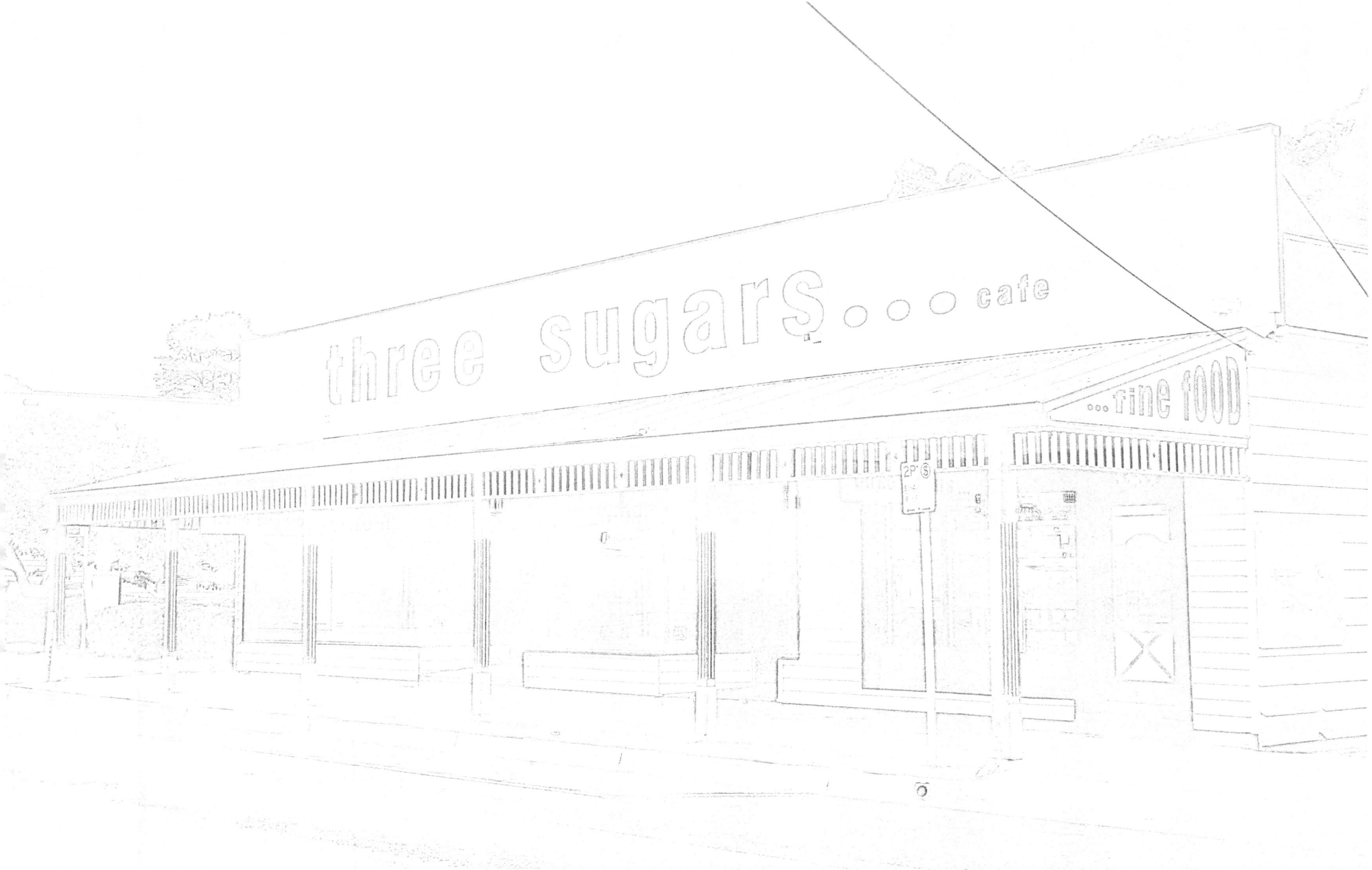
three sugars... cafe
...fine FOOD
2P

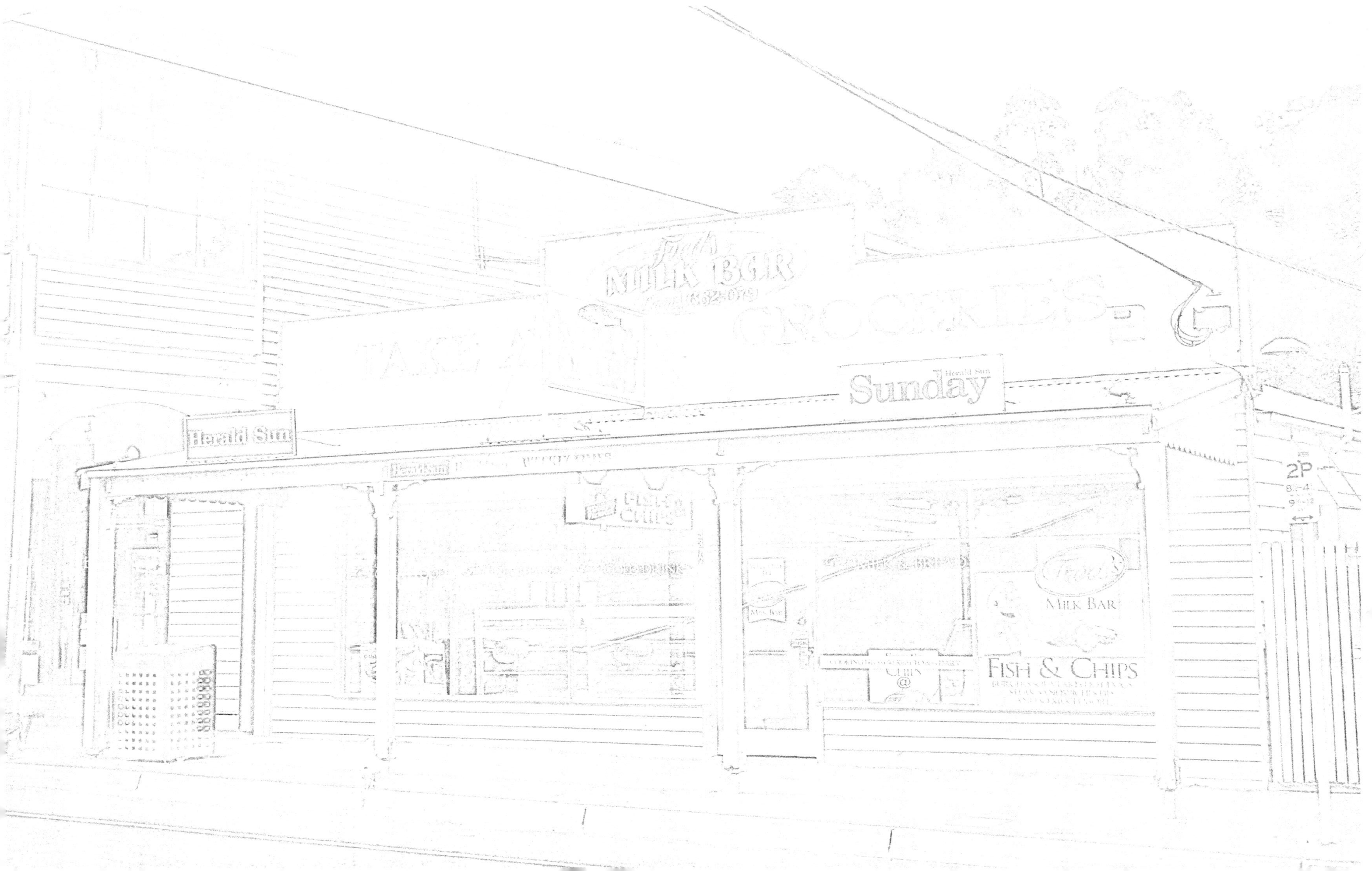
MILK BAR
Herald Sun
Sunday
Herald Sun
FISH & CHIPS
MILK BAR
FISH & CHIPS
2P

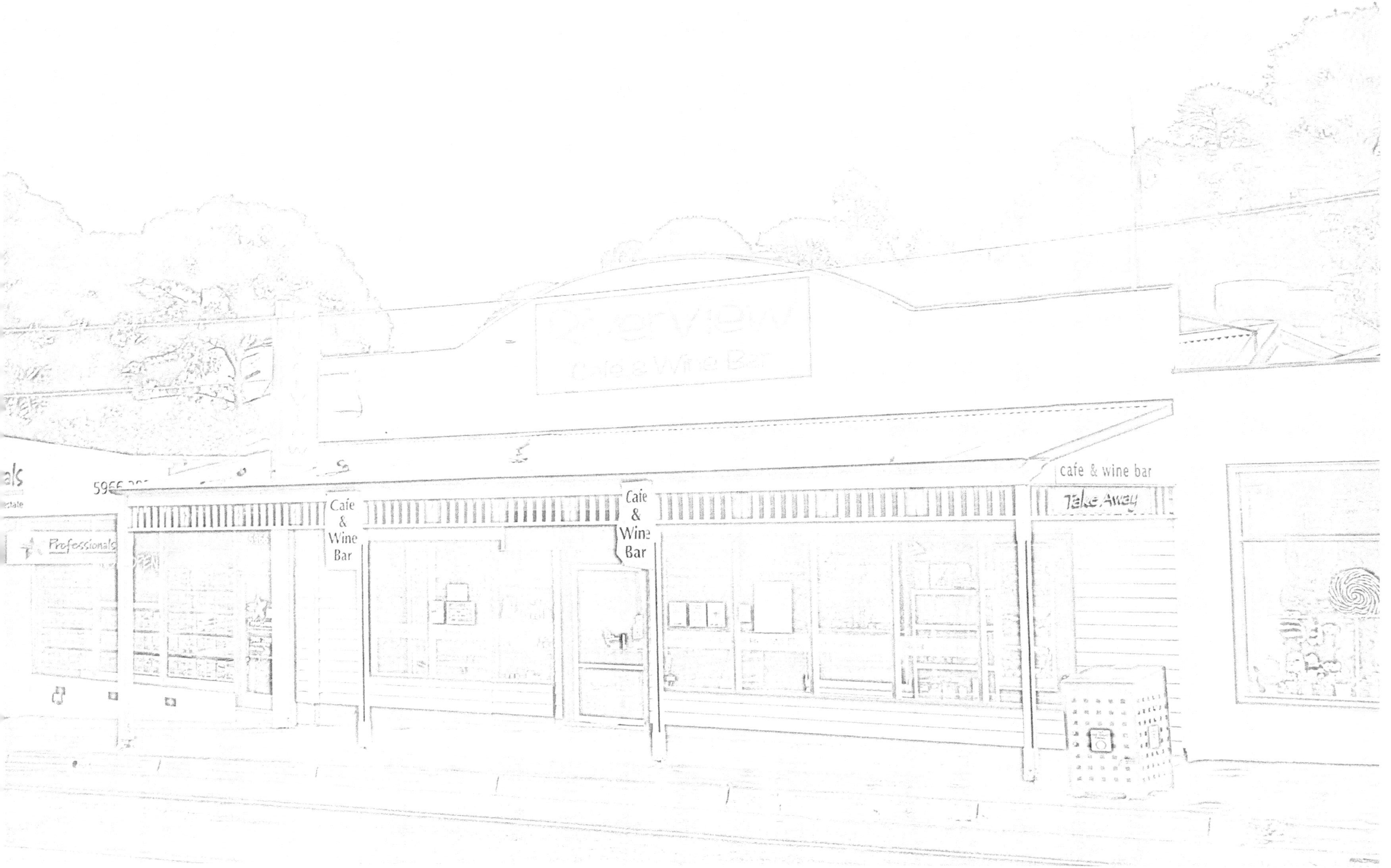

Cafe & Wine Bar
cafe & wine bar
Take Away
Cafe & Wine Bar
Cafe & Wine Bar
Professionals

HIGHFIELD RD
STATION RD

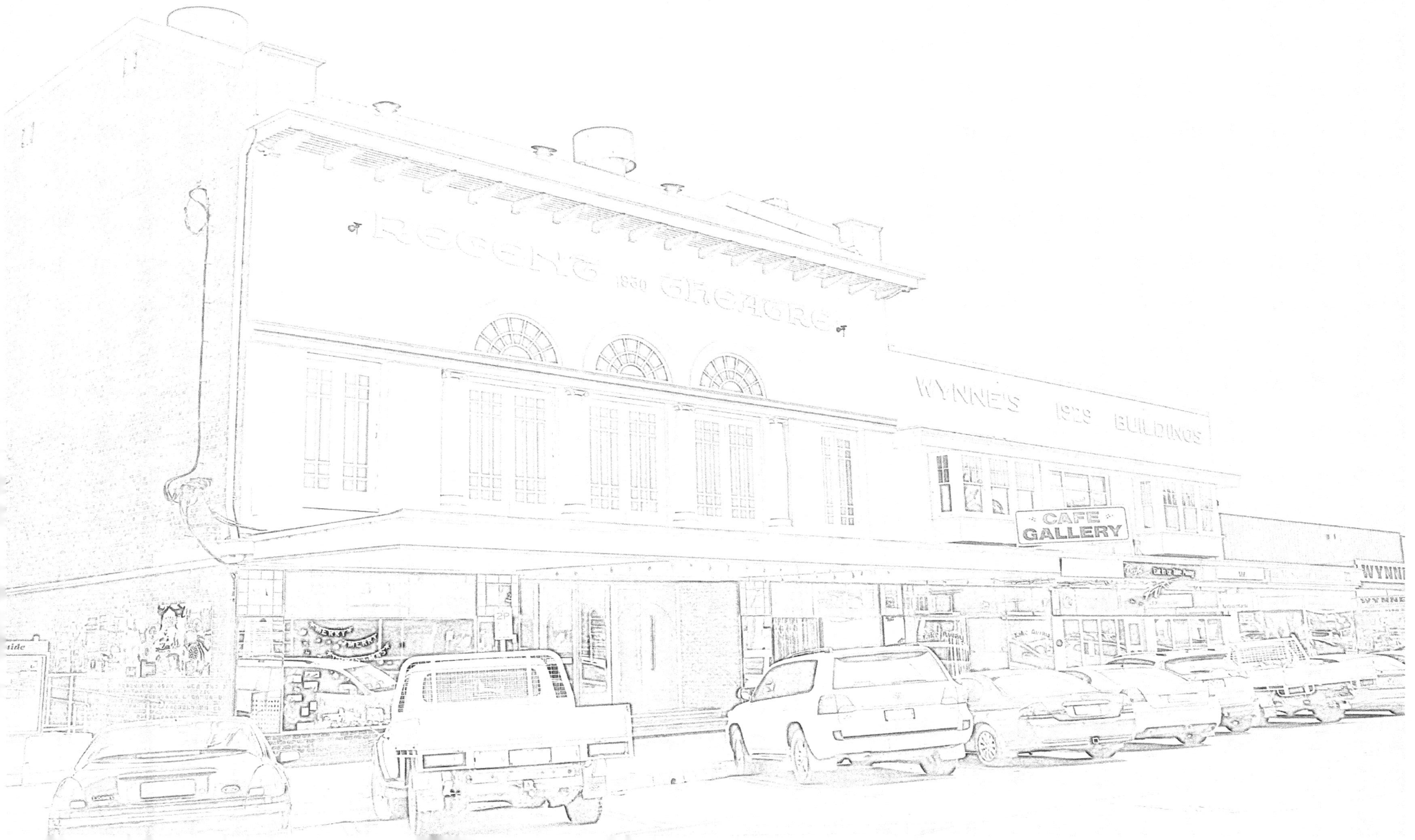
Regent 1850 Theatre
WYNNE'S 1929 BUILDINGS
CAFE GALLERY
WYNNE
MERRY
MERRY

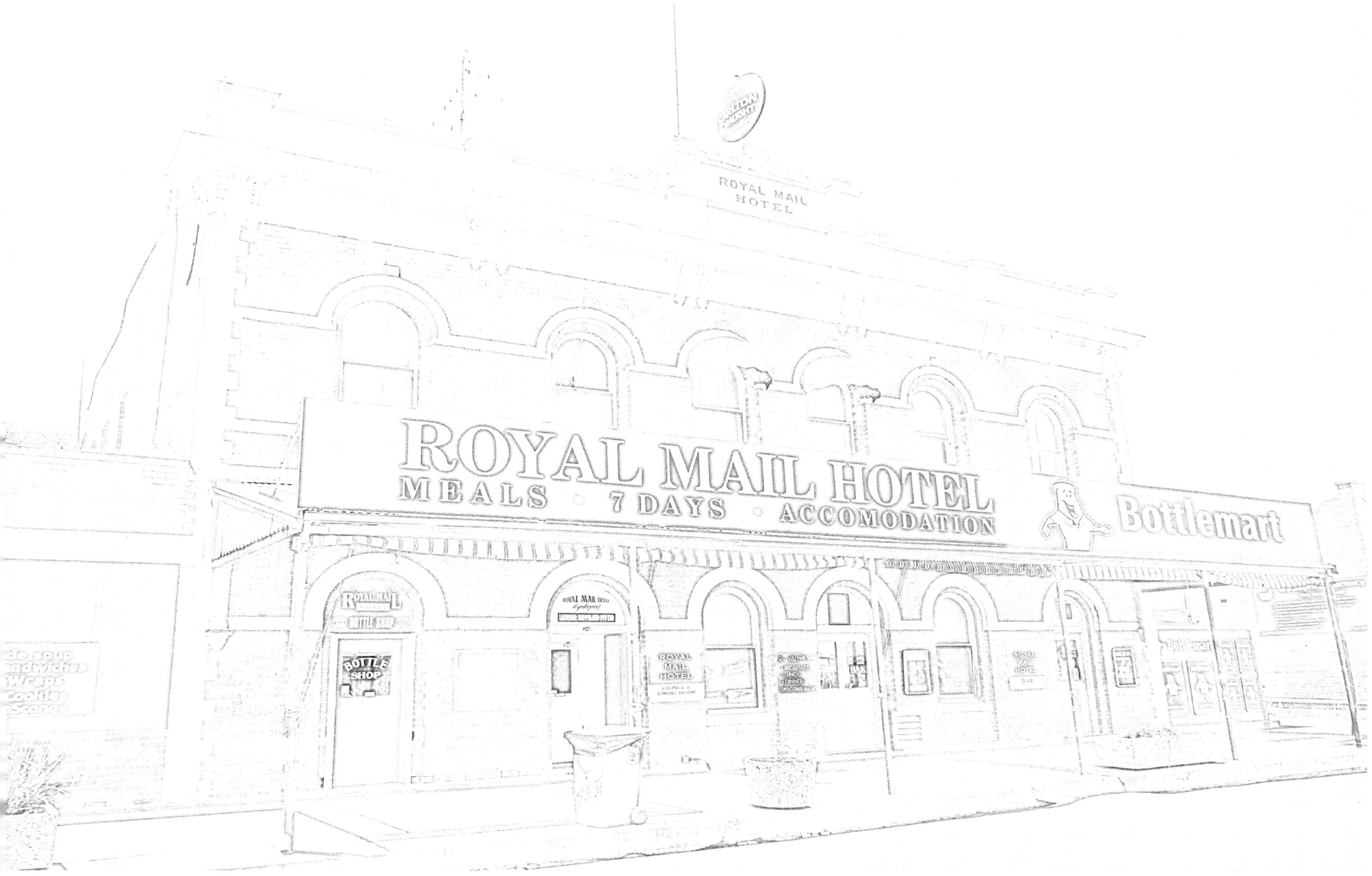
ROYAL MAIL
HOTEL
ROYAL MAIL HOTEL
MEALS • 7 DAYS • ACCOMODATION
Bottlemart
BOTTLE SHOP
ROYAL MAIL
HOTEL
LOUNGE &
DINING ROOM
ROYAL
MAIL
HOTEL
BAR

www.ingramcontent.com/pod-product-compliance
Lightning Source LLC
Chambersburg PA
CBHW081057180526
45170CB00005B/1790
* 9 7 8 0 3 5 9 8 6 5 2 1 5 *